Whole Food Asian Instant Pot Recipes:

Traditional and Healthy Asian Recipes for Pressure Cookers.

(+ 7-Days Asian Keto Diet Plan for Weight Loss!)

By

Henry Wilson

TABLE OF CONTENTS

INTRODUCTION

For beginner home cooks there is nothing more satisfying than cooking authentic and delicious Asian dishes within minutes. Whether you are craving a Thai, Japanese, Chinese, Vietnamese, or Korean dish or in the mood to try something new, this Asian Instant Pot cookbook teaches you all you need to make authentic Asian cuisine meals right at home! This Instant Pot cookbook will help you make Asian dishes in the comfort of your own kitchen, without hard-to-find ingredients or overly complicated instructions. Best of all – Instant Pot cooking makes sure your meal is ready within minutes. With the help of an Instant Pot, you can make authentic dishes that are healthier and tastier than their restaurant counterparts.

The recipes in this book will allow you to experience a wide variety of flavors: choose from chicken, beef, noodles, rice, curries, soup, stews, vegetarian, keto, and even desserts. This book helps readers find the perfect Asian dish for any occasion. This first-ever Asian Instant Pot Cookbook makes it easy to explore the culinary delights of Asian cuisine with easy recipes for hassle-free Instant Pot cooking. This Asian Instant Pot recipe book is sure to become the go-to book for home cooks interested in creating authentic and delicious Asian dishes at home. You can have fast, delicious Asian meals every day of the week! Join the Asian adventure and learn the unique style of Asian cooking in an Instant Pot. Click the Buy Now Button immediately!

CHAPTER 1 ASIAN CUISINE

Pakistani Cuisine

Pakistani cuisine is not well known, but the dishes are diverse and full of flavors. Pakistani cuisine is a blend of cooking tradition that includes Central Asia, the Indian subcontinent, and the Mughal dynasty. Main Pakistani dishes include biryani, nihari, keema, Haleem, naan, chicken jalfrezi, curry, chicken Karachi, seekh kebabs, kofta, and chicken tikka.

Indian Cuisine

Indian cuisine is one of the diverse cuisines of the world. Indian dishes vary according to the use of vegetables, grains, spices, fruits, and geographical location. India's cuisine evolved through cultural interactions with neighboring West Asia, Persia, Mongols, and ancient Greece. Famous Indian dishes include Butter chicken/ Murg Makhani, Tandoori chicken, Chicken tikka masala, red lamb, Malai kofta, chickpea curry, palak paneer, kaali daal, papdi chaat, naan, vindaloo, chicken biriyani, chicken tikka, kebabs, maili kofta, and more.

Indonesian Cuisine

Indonesian food is full of intense flavor and one of the most colorful and vibrant cuisines in the world. Indonesian cuisine offers a blend of Dutch, English, Spanish, Portuguese, Arab, Chinese and Indian dishes. Famous Indonesian dishes include Indonesian Satay, Beef Rendang, Fried rice, Nasi Rawon, Oxtail Soup, Siomay, Indomie, Nasi Uduk, Sweet Martabak, and Pempek.

Malaysian Cuisine

Malaysian cuisine reflects the multiethnic characteristics of its population. Malaysian cuisine is a melting pot of Indonesian, Chinese, European, Indian, and Middle Eastern dishes. Famous

Malaysian dishes include banana leaf, nasi Dagang, Bakuteh, Hokkien Mee, Sang, Har noodles, Satay, Nasi Kandar, Charsiew rice, Tanjung Tualang, Nasi Lemak, Hainanese chicken rice, beef rending and more.

Singaporean Cuisine

Singaporean cuisine is derived from several ethnic groups. Influences include the Chinese, Malays, Indonesian, Indian, and others such as Thailand, Eurasian, and the Middle East. Famous Singaporean dishes include Hainanese chicken rice, chili crab, laksa, Char Kuay Teow, Hokkien Prawn Mee, Barbecued Stingray, Fish Head Curry, Satay, Char Siew Rice/Noodles, and Oyster Omelette.

Thai Cuisine

In the 1980s, Thailand became a tourist hub and its cuisine become famous. Thai cuisine is one of the most popular cuisines in the world. Strong aromatic components, an abundance of spices and light preparation are the main features of Thai Cuisine. Popular Thai dishes include: Noodle soup, spicy shrimp soup, chicken in coconut soup, spicy green papaya salad, fried catfish with green mango salad, spicy seafood salad, spicy salad, stir-fried pumpkin, Thai style fried noodles, thick noodle dish, morning glory, fried rice, Thai curry, green curry, and more.

Vietnamese Cuisine

Vietnam is divided into 3 distinct sections: Southern, Central, and Northern. Each region differs in its main ingredients, flavors, and taste. However, they have a lot of things in common, such as soy sauce, shrimp paste, and fish sauce. Just like many Asian countries, Vietnamese cuisine emphasizes the balance of yin and yang. Famous Vietnamese dishes include Pho, Cha ca, Banh Mi, Banh Xeo, Goi Cuon, Mi Quang, Bun Thit Nuong, Com Tam, Banh Cuon, Xoi Xeo, Ca Kho To.

Filipino Cuisine

Filipino cuisine is composed of cuisines of various ethnolinguistic groups scattered around the Philippines. Filipino dishes employ three main tastes: sugar, salt, and vinegar. Famous Filipino dishes include Kinilaw, sinigang, kare-kare, Sisig, adobo, humba, lechon, pancit guisado, sinangag, balut, and Buko.

Chinese Cuisine

Chinese cuisine is as diverse as China. With over 5000 named dishes, Chinese cuisine is extremely varied. Traditionally, Chinese cuisine is meant to be enjoyed for its taste and texture, appearance and aroma, its nutritious properties, and balance and harmony of yin and yang elements. Popular dishes include Sweet and sour pork, Kung Pao Chicken, Ma Po Tofu, Wontons, Dumplings, Chow Mein, Peking Roasted Duck, and Spring Rolls.

Japanese Cuisine

Japanese cuisine incorporates the traditional and regional foods of Japan, which have developed through centuries of social, economic, and political changes. There are so many unique and fascinating Japanese dishes and they are becoming popular to the West over recent years. Favorite dishes include Sushi & Sashimi, Ramen, Tempura, Kare-Raisu, Okonomiyaki, Shabu Shabu, Miso Soup, Yakitori, Onigiri, Udon, Soba, Gyudon, and Gyoza.

Korean Cuisine

Korean cuisine refers to the traditional foods and preparation techniques of Korea. Korean food has an emphasis on fermented vegetable kimchi, cooked meat without much oil, and vegetables, and considered as one of the healthiest food on earth. Popular foods include Kimchi, mixed rice, marinated beef barbecue, stir-fried noodles, sweet syrupy pancakes, spicy rice cake, ox bone soup, soft tofu stew, pork strips, seafood vegetable pancake, pumpkin porridge, cold buckwheat noodles, blood sausage, and ginseng chicken soup.

CHAPTER 2 ASIAN SPICES

Let's learn about widely used Asian spices:

1. Chilies: Chilies are used widely in Asian cooking. There are small chilies, medium chilies, large chilies, and bird's eye chilies.

2. Chinese chives: Chinese chives are more pungent than European chives.

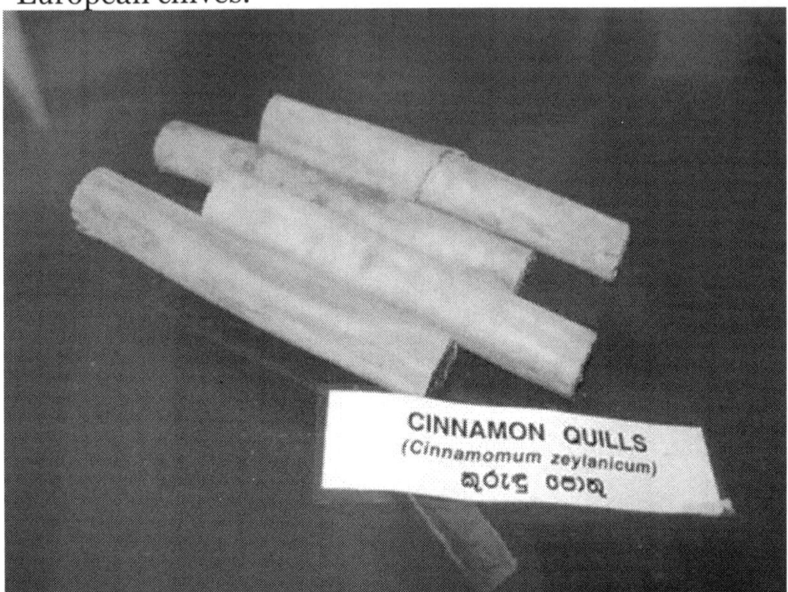

3. Cinnamon: Cinnamon sold in American markets is usually cassia bark. True cinnamon is from Sri Lanka.

4. Fresh coriander/cilantro: Coriander is used widely in Asian cuisine. The leaves, stalks, and roots, all are used in cooking.

5. Curry leaves: They are an essential part of Indian cooking.

6. Fenugreek: Fresh leaves are used extensively.

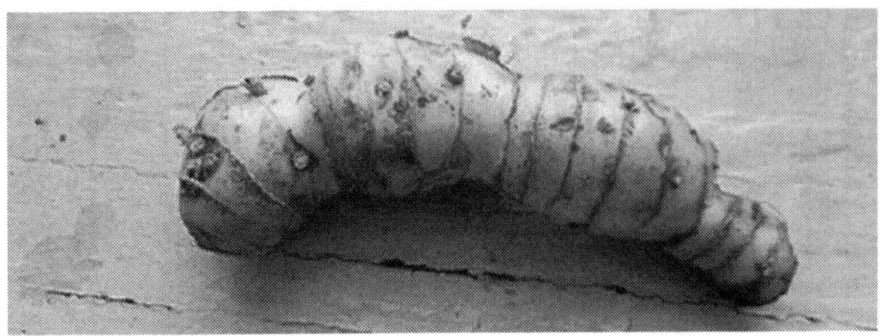

7. Galangal: They look like ginger but different.

8. Ginger: Ginger is a popular cooking ingredient in Asian cooking.

9. Kaffir lime leaves: These leaves widely used in Thai cooking

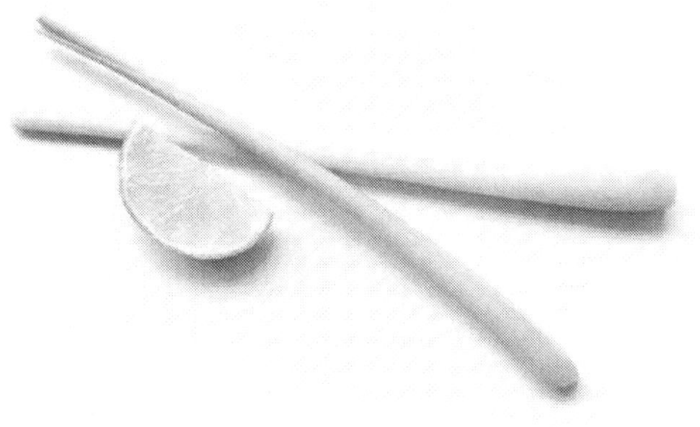

10. Lemongrass: Lemongrass is an essential cooking component.

11. Star anise: You can use them whole or ground.

12. Thai basil: They are used widely in Thai cooking.

13. Green cardamom: This spice adds a subtler flavor to a dish.

14. Cloves: They are used in many parts of Asia.

15. Ground coriander: The seed form is popular in Asian cooking.

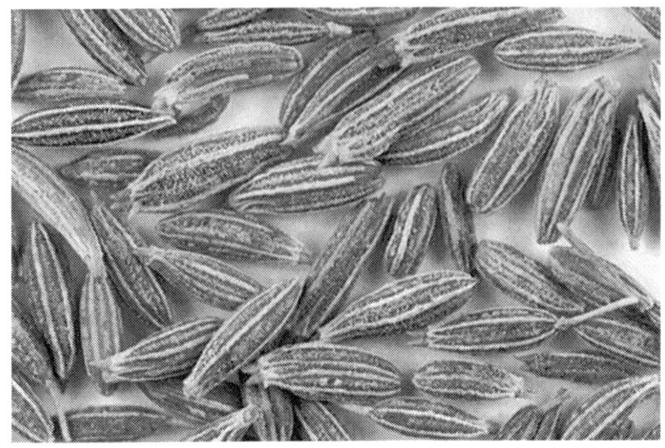

16. Cumin: There are two types of cumin black and white. White cumin is commonly used in Southeast Asia.

17. Fenugreek seeds: They are a popular spice ingredient.

18. Five spice: Five-spice contains cloves, anise pepper, fennel seeds, star anise, and cassia.

19. Nigella: Nigella is black cumin.

20. Seven-spice: Seven-spice is known as Japanese shichimi.

21. Turmeric: Turmeric adds a distinctive flavor to Asian dishes.

CHAPTER 3, 7-DAY MEAL PLAN

Weekly Meal Planner

	Breakfast	Lunch	Dinner	Dessert
Sunday	Chicken Noodle Soup (Pho Ga)	Chicken Tikka Masala	Indian Coconut Shrimp Curry	Tofu Pudding
Monday	Pilipino Chicken Florentine	Chinese Pork Salad	Chicken Biryani	Sweet Rice Cake
Tuesday	Asian Chicken and Rice	Chicken Adobo	Indonesian Chicken Noodle Soup	Watalappan
Wednesday	Filipino Beef Tapa	Coconut Fish Curry	Mongolian Chicken	Rice Pudding
Thursday	Fish Congee (Chao ca)	Korean Pork Ribs	Indonesian Curry Chicken	Leche Flan
Friday	Fish Biryani	Coconut Chicken Curry	Beef Rendang	New Year Cake
Saturday	Chinese Sticky Rice	Vietnamese Salmon	Vietnamese Caramel Salmon	Sponge Cake

CHAPTER 4 CHICKEN RECIPES

Here is a classic Asian recipe. Chicken tikka masala. Enjoy a popular Asian meal without leaving your home.

Chicken Tikka Masala (Indian)

Cook time: 20 minutes	Servings: 2

Ingredients for marinating

- Boneless, skinless chicken – ½ lb. chopped into smaller pieces
- Greek yogurt – ½ cup
- Garam masala – 1 ½ tsps.
- Lemon juice – 1 ½ tsps.
- Black pepper – ½ tsp.
- Ground ginger – ¼ tsp.

For the sauce

- Canned tomato puree – 7 ounces
- Garlic – 2 cloves, minced
- Garam masala – 2 tsps.
- Paprika – ¼ tsp.
- Turmeric – ¼ tsp.
- Salt – ¼ tsp.
- Cayenne to taste
- Heavy whipping cream – ½ cup

For serving

- Basmati rice
- Naan
- Freshly chopped cilantro

Method

1. Except for the chicken, combine all the marinade ingredients in a bowl and mix well.
2. Add chicken chunks and coat well. Marinate in the refrigerator for at least 1 hour.
3. Press the sauté mode on your Instant Pot (IP).

4. Add the chicken and marinade. Sauté until 5 minutes or cooked on all side. Stirring occasionally. Turn off the sauté mode.
5. Except for the cream, add all the sauce ingredients to the IP, pour over the chicken.
6. Cover and cook at high pressure for 10 minutes at manual.
7. Release pressure when cooked.
8. Add the cream and mix. Simmer on sauté for a few minutes.
9. Serve with basmati rice or naan.

Nutritional Facts Per Serving

- Calories: 460
- Fat: 27g
- Carb: 19g
- Protein: 32g

With traditional stovetop cooking, these flavorful recipes need hours to cook. With Instant Pot, can enjoy this rich and complex dish within a few minutes.

Vietnamese Chicken Noodle Soup (Pho Ga)

Cook time: 30 minutes	Servings: 2

Ingredients

- Canola oil – 1 tbsp.
- Yellow onion – 1 medium, halved
- Ginger – 1-inch, sliced
- Coriander seeds – ½ tbsp.
- Star anise pods – 2
- Cloves – 3
- Cinnamon – ½ stick
- Cardamom pods – 1, smashed

- Bone-in, skin-on chicken thighs – 3
- Fish sauce – 1 ½ tbsps.
- Sugar – ½ tbsp.
- Water – 4 cups
- Kosher salt to taste
- Black pepper to taste
- Rice noodles – 2 servings, cooked

For toppings

- Sliced jalapeno, lime wedges, fresh herbs and sliced scallions (to taste)

Method

1. Press Sauté to preheat the Instant Pot.
2. Add oil to the hot pot. Add ginger, onions and cook for 4 minutes or until charred. Don't stir.
3. Add the cardamom, cinnamon, cloves, star anise, and coriander. Stir and cook for 1 minute.
4. Add the sugar, sauce, and chicken. Add water and cover.
5. Press Manual and cook on high pressure for 15 minutes.
6. Once cooked, do a natural release for 10 minutes.
7. Remove the chicken and strain the broth.
8. Season with salt and pepper.
9. Arrange the chicken with cooked noodles in 4 bowls.
10. Pour over the broth and garnish with toppings.
11. Serve.

Nutritional Facts Per Serving

- Calories: 620
- Fat: 8g

- Carb: 57g
- Protein: 25g

The epitome of a one-pot meal is chicken biryani. This dish is made with tender chicken, aromatic basmati rice, herbs, and spices. Chicken biryani is one of the favorite dishes in India, Pakistan, and Bangladesh.

Chicken Biryani (Indian & Pakistani)

Cook time: 40 minutes	Servings: 2

Ingredients

- Garam masala – ½ tsp.
- Ginger – ¼ tbsp. grated
- Garlic – ¼ tbsp. minced

- Red chili powder – ¼ tbsp.
- Turmeric – a pinch
- Mint leaves – a few
- Chopped cilantro - a few
- Lemon juice – ½ tbsp.
- Plain yogurt – 1 tbsp.
- Kosher salt – ½ tsp.
- Chicken – ½ pound, bone-in, skinless (cut into bite-sized pieces)

Remaining ingredients

- Basmati rice – ¾ cup, extra-long variety (washed and soaked in water)
- Ghee – ¾ tbsp. divided
- Yellow onion – ½, sliced
- Bay leaves- 1
- Salt – ½ tsp.
- Saffron – ¼ tsp. mixed in 1 tbsp. warm milk
- Eggs - 1 ½ boiled and shelled
- Jalapeno – ¼, sliced

Raita

- Plain yogurt – ½ cup
- Yellow onion – ¼, finely diced
- Tomato – ½ diced
- Kosher salt to taste
- Chopped cilantro – ¼ tsp.

Method

1. In a bowl, add the mint leaves, turmeric, chili powder, garlic, ginger, garam masala, half of the lemon juice, chopped cilantro, salt, and yogurt.

2. Add chicken and coat well. Marinate in the refrigerator for at least 30 minutes.
3. Press sauté and add ghee and onions to the hot pot.
4. Cook for 10 minutes or until the onion is caramelized.
5. Remove and set aside about half of the onion for garnishing.
6. Add the rest of the ghee to the Instant Pot and add sliced jalapeno.
7. Add half of the marinated chicken, marinated liquid and bay leaf to the pot. Press Cancel and mix well. Deglaze the pot with a spatula and remove all the brown bits from bottom of the pot by scraping.
8. Add the remaining chicken and close the lid.
9. Press Manual and cook for 4 minutes on High.
10. Do a quick release, and open.
11. Mix the chicken well and remove any stuck food from the bottom.
12. Drain the rice and add to the chicken. Add 1 cup of water and salt. Adjust water if necessary.
13. Close and cook on Manual on High for 6 minutes.
14. Do a quick release when cooked.
15. Open and gently mix the rice and chicken.
16. Garnish with saffron liquid and caramelized onions
17. Serve with lemon wedges, hard-boiled egg, and Raita.
18. To make the Raita: in a bowl, whisk the yogurt. Add salt, tomatoes, and onion and mix well. Garnish with cilantro.

Nutritional Facts Per Serving

- Calories: 503
- Fat: 18g
- Carb: 60g
- Protein: 20g

This Malaysian ginger soy chicken is delicious and takes only 8 minutes to cook. Ginger gives an amazing aroma to the dish and soy sauce and sweet soy sauce complements the flavor.

Ginger Soy Chicken

Cook time: 8 minutes	Servings: 2

Ingredients

- Chicken – 1 lb. (wings drummettes and wingettes and drumsticks) chopped into pieces
- Oil – ¾ tbsp.
- Ginger – ¾ inch, sliced

- Soy sauce – 1 1/3 tbsps.
- Sweet soy sauce – 2 tbsps.
- Ground white pepper – 2 dashes
- Water – ½ cup
- Sesame oil – ½ tsp.
- Scallion – 2/3 stalk, sliced

Method

1. Press sauté on the Instant Pot.
2. Add oil to the hot pot.
3. Add chicken and sear until slightly brown.
4. Add the ginger and sauté a little bit.
5. Add the sesame oil, ground pepper, sweet soy sauce, soy sauce, and water.
6. Cover and press Manual Cook 8 minutes on High pressure.
7. Do a quick release.
8. Open and stir in scallion.
9. Serve.

Nutritional Facts Per Serving

- Calories: 400
- Fat: 16.7g
- Carb: 19.8g
- Protein: 43g

This Malaysian chicken dish with sticky sweet and savory honey sauce will be your family favorite. If you love moist, juicy, soft, and tender chicken thighs in sauce this meal is for you.

Honey Sesame Chicken

Cook time: 8 minutes	Servings: 2

Ingredients

- Boneless, skinless chicken thighs – 0.75 lbs.
- Salt and ground pepper to taste
- Oil – ¾ tbsp.

- Garlic – 1 clove, minced
- Toasted white sesame – ½ tsp.
- Chopped scallion - ½ tbsp.

Honey sesame sauce

- Chicken broth – ¼ cup
- Honey – 1 ¼ tbsps.
- Soy sauce – 1 tbsp.
- Dark soy sauce – ¼ tsp.
- Apple cider vinegar – ½ tbsp.
- Sriracha – ½ tsp.
- Sesame oil – ½ tsp.
- Corn starch – ½ tsp.

Method

1. Season the chicken with salt and pepper. Set aside.
2. Mix all the sauce ingredients together. Make sure the corn starch and honey are mixed completely. Set aside.
3. Press sauté on your Instant Pot.
4. Add the cooking oil.
5. Sear chicken on all sides.
6. Add the garlic and sauté for a minute.
7. Pour in the sauce and add sesame.
8. Cover and press Manual.
9. Cook on High pressure for 8 minutes.
10. Do a quick release.
11. Add chopped scallion and serve.

Nutritional Facts Per Serving

- Calories: 302
- Fat: 12.8g
- Carb: 13.2g
- Protein: 34.3g

This chicken recipe is a simplified version of traditional Filipino comfort foot. An Instant Pot cooks it in no time at all and one pot means less time to clean.

Pilipino Chicken Adobo

Cook time: 25 minutes	Servings: 2

Ingredients

- Chicken legs – 2, thighs and drumsticks separated
- Salt and pepper to taste
- Vegetable oil – 1 tbsp.
- Soy sauce – 2 tbsps.
- Sugar - 1 tbsp.
- White distilled vinegar – 1 tbsp.

- Garlic – 2 cloves, smashed
- Bay leaves – 1
- Yellow onion – 1/2, sliced
- Scallions -1, sliced
- Cooked rice for serving

Method

1. Season the chicken with salt and pepper.
2. Press Sauté on your Instant Pot and add the oil.
3. Add half the chicken and brown on both sides, about 7 minutes.
4. Remove to a plate and brown the remaining chicken pieces.
5. Return the chicken to the pot and add the onion, bay leaves, garlic, vinegar, sugar, soy sauce, and pepper.
6. Cover with the lid and cook on High for 8 minutes.
7. Do a quick release and open the lid.
8. Press sauté and reduce the sauce for about 20 minutes, or until the sauce is dark brown and fragrant.
9. Arrange on serving plates.
10. Sprinkle with scallions and serve with rice.

Nutritional Facts Per Serving

- Calories: 424
- Fat: 27.1g
- Carb: 11.7g
- Protein: 32g

This is a Filipino dish made with potatoes, peas, bell peppers, carrots, and chicken.

Chicken Afritada

Cook time: 35 minutes	Servings: 2

Ingredients

- Chicken drumsticks and thighs – 4 pieces
- Garlic – 1 tbsp. minced
- Onion – ½ sliced
- Tomato paste – 4 ounces
- Chicken broth – ½ cup
- Soy sauce – 1 tbsp.
- Fish sauce – 1 tbsp.

- Dried bay leave – 1
- Carrots – 2, chopped
- Potato – 1, diced
- Bell pepper – ¼, sliced
- Frozen peas – 1 tbsp.
- Cornstarch – ½ tbsp. mixed in cold water (optional)

Method

1. Press sauté and oil and brown the chicken on all sides.
2. Add onion and garlic.
3. Remove the chicken from the pot.
4. Add broth and deglaze the pot. Remove all stuck bits from the bottom of the pot.
5. Add tomato paste, bay leaves, fish sauce, and soy sauce to the pot. Mix well. Return the browned chicken to the pot.
6. Close the lid and press poultry, cook for 10 minutes.
7. Do a quick release and open the lid.
8. Add peas, bell pepper, potato, and carrots.
9. Cook on Manual for 1 minute.
10. Do a quick release and open.
11. Taste and season if necessary.
12. Serve.

Nutritional Facts Per Serving

- Calories: 315
- Fat: 3.6g
- Carb: 40.5g
- Protein: 31.5g

After a hard day's work, you may not find you have much energy, but you will find time to cook this delicious chicken dish. Once you have tasted this dish, you will never buy that frozen pre-made pasta again.

Pilipino Chicken Florentine

Cook time: 20 minutes	Servings: 2

Ingredients

- Boneless chicken – 1 lb.
- Oil – 1 tbsp.
- Onion powder – 1 tbsp.
- Garlic powder – 1 tbsp.
- Tie Noodles – ½ box
- Cream of mushroom soup - 1 can

- Milk – ¾ cup
- Fresh spinach – 1 cup
- Salt and pepper to taste

Method

1. Press sauté on your pressure cooker.
2. Add oil, then brown chicken on all sides.
3. Add the garlic, onion, and season with salt and pepper. Mix well.
4. Add the cream of mushroom soup.
5. Top with noodles, then add the milk and sprinkle with pepper.
6. Close and cook 15 minutes on Manual.
7. Do a quick release and open.
8. Stir everything and shred the chicken.
9. Stir in the fresh spinach and mix.
10. Serve.

Nutritional Facts Per Serving

- Calories: 412
- Fat: 15g
- Carb: 36.3g
- Protein: 32.5g

This Instant Pot Mongolian chicken dish takes only 30 minutes to cook. The dish produces flavorful, juicy and tender chicken

Mongolian Chicken

Cook time: 20 minutes	Servings: 2

Ingredients

- Boneless skinless chicken breasts - 1 1/3, cut into cubes
- Extra virgin olive oil – 2/3 tbsps.
- Brown sugar – ½ tbsp. or to taste

- Garlic – 1 clove, minced
- Fresh ginger – ½ tsp. minced
- Soy sauce – ½ tbsp.
- Broth – 1/6 cup
- Carrots – 2 tbsps.
- Red pepper flakes – ½ tsp.
- Garlic powder – 1/3 tbsp.

Cornstarch slurry

- Cornstarch – 2/3 tbsp.

Optional

- Green onion – 1 tbsp.
- Sesame seeds – to taste

Rice

- Basmati rice – 2/3 cup
- Water – 2/3 cup
- Butter – 2/3 tbsp.
- Salt – 1 pinch

Method

1. Press sauté on your Instant Pot.
2. Add oil.
3. Add chicken and sauté for 2 to 3 minutes. Stir constantly.
4. Deglaze the pot if necessary.
5. Add red pepper flakes, garlic powder, carrot, water, brown sugar, soy sauce, garlic, and ginger to the pot.
6. Stir to mix.
7. Rice: Add the rice, salt, and water in a pot.
8. Stir to combine.
9. Add a trivet to the instant pot and place the rice pot onto the trivet.

10. Cover with aluminum foil and pinch a few times with a fork.
11. Close and cook at High for 5 minutes.
12. Do a natural release.
13. Open the lid and remove the pot with the rice.
14. Rest and fluff the rice with a fork.
15. Press sauté.
16. In a bowl, combine water and cornstarch, whisk to mix.
17. Add the mixture to the pot and stir to combine.
18. Sauté for a few minutes without the lid.
19. Turn of the heat.
20. Garnish and serve.

Nutritional Facts Per Serving

- Calories: 538
- Fat: 11g
- Carb: 84g
- Protein: 24g

This is a hearty Instant Pot meal with an Asian twist. It is perfect for a lunch or a dinner dish.

Asian Chicken and Rice

Cook time: 10 minutes	Servings: 2

Ingredients

- Uncooked jasmine rice – ½ cup (drained and rinsed)
- Skinless chicken thighs – 2, boneless
- Salt – ¼ tsp.
- Ground black pepper – 1 pinch
- Peanut oil – ½ tbsp.

- Yellow onion – ¼, chopped
- Minced garlic – 1 ½ cloves
- Minced ginger – 1 tsp.
- Cumin powder – 1 tsp.
- Chicken broth – ½ cup
- Carrot – 1, chopped
- Bell pepper – ½ chopped
- Soy sauce – ½ tbsp.
- Sesame oil – ½ tsp.
- Chopped green onion – 1 tbsp. for garnish

Method

1. Season the chicken with salt and pepper. Marinate for 10 to 15 minutes.
2. Add peanut oil in the Instant Pot.
3. Press Sauté and place onion in the pot.
4. Stir fry for 3 minutes.
5. Add the cumin, ginger, and garlic. Cook until fragrant.
6. Turn off sauté and add broth.
7. Deglaze the pot if necessary.
8. Add the pepper and carrot.
9. Spread the rice in the pot evenly.
10. Top with chicken. And drizzle with soy sauce. Don't stir.
11. Close and press Manual.
12. Cook on High for 10 minutes.
13. Release pressure naturally.
14. Shred the chicken with forks.
15. Drizzle with sesame oil.
16. Add the sesame seed and green onions.
17. Mix and serve.

Nutritional Facts Per Serving

- Calories: 417
- Fat: 10.9g
- Carb: 46g
- Protein: 32g

CHAPTER 5 MEAT RECIPES

This is a moist and tender pressure cooker Chinese BBQ pork. This sweet and savory dish goes great with noodles or rice.

Chinese BBQ Pork (CHAR SIU)

Cook time: 45 minutes	Servings: 2

Ingredients

- Pork butt meat – 1 pound, split the longer side in half

- Honey – 3 tbsp.
- Light soy sauce – 2 tbsps.
- Water – 1 cup
- Kosher salt to taste

Marinade

- Chu Hou pastes – 1 tbsp.
- Chinese fermented red bean curd – 2 cubes
- Char siu sauce – 3 tbsps.
- Sesame oil – ½ tsp.
- Shaoxing wine – 2 tbsps.
- Garlic powder – 1 tsp.
- Light soy sauce -1 tbsp.

Method

1. Make lots of deep holes in the meat with a fork.
2. Marinade the pork for up to 2 hours in a Ziploc bag.
3. Remove the pork and marinade from the bag. Add 1 cup water in the Ziploc bag and mix to get the remaining marinade.
4. Add the marinade mixture into the pressure cooker.
5. Place the meat in the pressure cooker on a steamer basket.
6. Season the meat with salt on both sides.
7. Cover with the lid and cook on high pressure for 18 minutes.
8. Then do a natural release for 12 minutes.
9. In a bowl, mix honey and 2 tbsp. soy sauce.
10. Brush the meat with this mixture.
11. Preheat the oven to 450F.
12. Place pork in the oven and cook until both sides are browned, about 4 to 6 minutes.
13. Serve over noodles or rice with leftover sauce.

Nutritional Facts Per Serving

- Calories: 804
- Fat: 58.3g
- Carb: 40.1g
- Protein: 27.3g

This Korean meat dish is accentuated by black pepper, fresh ginger, green chili pepper, and shishito pepper. It is a childhood favorite for most Koreans.

Korean Pork Ribs (Dwaeji Galbi Jjim)

Cook time: 25 minutes	Servings: 2

Ingredients

- Pork ribs - ¾ lb. fat trimmed and cut into pieces
- Soy sauce – 65 ml. (jin ganjang)
- Water – ½ cup

- Green chili peppers (Korean) – 2, cut into pieces
- Shishito peppers – 3 to 4, chopped
- Fresh ginger – 1/3 oz. chopped
- Black pepper – 1/6 tsp.

Method

1. Soak ribs in cold water for 10 minutes.
2. In the Instant Pot, add soy sauce, water, ribs, ginger, black pepper, and ½ the green peppers.
3. Close and press Meat/Stew. Cook for reduced time – 20 minutes.
4. Release pressure when cooked.
5. Oven and add rest of the chili peppers and all the shishito peppers.
6. Close the pot again and cook on manual at low pressure for 5 minutes.
7. Serve.

Nutritional Facts Per Serving

- Calories: 301
- Fat: 17g
- Carb: 1g
- Protein: 30g

This Chinese dish is made with fermented soybeans, black beans, and pork ribs. This dish is fuss-free, super easy and fork tender delicious.

Pork Ribs with Black Beans (Chinese)

Cook time: 50 minutes	Servings: 2

Ingredients

- Pork ribs – 2/3 lbs. cut into bite size pieces
- Shao Hsing cooking wine – ½ tbsp.
- Salt to taste
- Ginger – 15 g, minced
- Garlic – 1 clove, minced

- Red chili – ½, seeded and minced
- Fermented black beans – 25 g, minced
- Fermented soybeans – 15 g, minced
- Sugar – ¼ tsp.
- Sesame oil – ½ tsp.
- Water – 1 ½ cups

Method

1. In a bowl, combine the salt, wine and pork ribs.
2. Place minced soybeans, black beans, red chili, garlic, and ginger and stir in sugar. Pour mixture over pork rib pieces. Coat well and marinate for 30 minutes.
3. Add water to the Pressure Cooker and drizzle sesame oil over the ribs.
4. Cover the bowl with a piece of aluminum foil.
5. Place bowl on a steaming rack.
6. Transfer the rack into the pressure cooker pot.
7. Close and lock the lid.
8. Press Steam and set time for 50 minutes.
9. Once finished cooking, allow the cooker to Keep Warm.
10. Press Cancel after 10 minutes and release pressure naturally.
11. Serve.

Nutritional Facts Per Serving

- Calories: 268
- Fat: 13.2g
- Carb: 8.2g
- Protein: 25.1g

When traveling to Vietnam, you won't find this delicious pork belly dish in many Vietnamese restaurants. However, every Vietnamese family makes this dish at home. Cooking this dish is a part of the Lunar New Year celebration.

Vietnamese Braised Pork Belly (Thit Kho tau)

Cook time: 35 minutes	Servings: 2

Ingredients

- Lean pork belly - ¾ lb. cut into 1-inch squares
- Large eggs – 3 (semi-soft boiled and peeled)
- Garlic – 1 clove, minced
- Shallot – ½, diced

- Fish sauce – ½ tbsp.
- Coconut water – 1 cup
- Granulated sugar – 2 tbsps.
- Ground black pepper – ¼ tsp.
- Kosher salt to taste
- Soy sauce – ½ tsp.
- Thai chili pepper for garnish

Method

1. In a bowl, add the pork belly pieces, black pepper, salt, soy sauce, shallot, garlic, and fish sauce. Mix and coat the meat well and set aside.
2. To make the sauce: add the sugar into the Instant Pot and press Sauté.
3. Melt the sugar and let it caramelize, about 5 minutes.
4. Once the sauce takes a coffee color, add the marinated meat and sauté for 5 minutes. Stir and coat well. Add the coconut water and stir. Turn off the sauté mode.
5. Press Manual and cook on high pressure for 35 minutes.
6. Once cooked, do a natural release for 15 minutes.
7. Open the lid and the eggs.
8. Cover and press Keep Warm.
9. Wait about 15 minutes so the eggs can absorb the flavor of the dish.
10. Skim the fat from the sauce.
11. Serve the dish with steamed vegetables and/or rice.
12. Garnish with Thai chilis.

Nutritional Facts Per Serving

- Calories: 428

- Fat: 13.3g
- Carb: 26.9g
- Protein: 51g

This is fall-apart tender, delicious, Malaysian Instant Pot Beef Rendang. With the traditional cooking method, this recipe usually takes several hours. but without Instant Pot, this recipe takes only a few minutes.

Malaysian Beef Rendang

Cook time: 30 minutes	Servings: 2

Ingredients

- Onion – ½ cup, chopped
- Minced garlic – ½ tbsp.
- Minced ginger – ½ tbsp.
- Jalapeno – ½
- Vegetable oil – 1 tbsp.

- Rendang curry paste – ½ package
- Skirt steak – ½ pound, cut into 2-inch chunks
- Water – ½ cup, divided
- Full-fat coconut milk – ½ cup, divided
- Shredded coconut – 1 tbsp.

Method

1. Press sauté and add oil to the hot pot.
2. Add the vegetables and stir to coat with oil.
3. Add the rendang paste and stir. Roast the paste for 3 to 4 minutes.
4. Add the steak and stir to coat with spices, about 2 minutes.
5. Pour in ¼ cup water and deglaze the pot well. Remove any burned bits.
6. Add half the coconut milk and remaining water.
7. Cook on High pressure for 25 minutes.
8. Do a natural release for 10 minutes.
9. Open the lid and add the remaining coconut milk and mix well.
10. Garnish with shredded coconut and serve.

Nutritional Facts Per Serving

- Calories: 391
- Fat: 29g
- Carb: 7g
- Protein: 26g

This Instant Pot Beef Caldereta is your go-to dish if you are looking for a faster way to cook and enjoy Filipino food.

Beef Caldereta

Cook time: 45 minutes	Servings: 2

Ingredients

- Extra virgin olive oil – ½ tbsp.
- Unsalted butter – ½ tbsp.
- Beef short ribs – 1 pound, cut in pieces
- Worcestershire sauce – 1 tbsp.
- Garlic – 2 cloves, minced
- Onion – ½, sliced
- Bell pepper – 1, seeded and sliced
- Tomato paste – 3 ounces

- Canned liver spread – 2 tbsps.
- Beef broth – 1 cup
- Potato – 1, quartered
- Pitted Spanish green olives with pimiento – 2 tbsps.
- Red pepper flakes – ½ tsp.
- Salt – ½ tsp.
- Ground black pepper – ¼ tsp.

Method

1. Press the sauté on your Instant Pot.
2. Add oil and butter.
3. Braise the beef short ribs and brown on all sides.
4. Drizzle with Worcestershire sauce.
5. Add the bell peppers, onions, and garlic and stir and cook for 2 minutes.
6. Turn off the sauté mode.
7. Add the liver spread and tomato paste. Pour the beef broth.
8. Add the olives and potato. Season with salt, pepper, and red pepper flakes.
9. Cover and cook on High pressure for 45 minutes.
10. Do a quick release when done.
11. Serve.

Nutritional Facts Per Serving

- Calories: 472
- Fat: 18.6g
- Carb: 33.9g
- Protein: 42.5g

This is a Filipino style BBQ rib recipe. It is so easy to make, and you can make them sweet or savory.

Filipino BBQ Ribs

Cook time: 45 minutes	Servings: 2

Ingredients

- Spare ribs – ½ rack, cut into portions
- Filipino soy sauce – 2 tbsp.
- Lemon juice – 1 tbsp.
- Ketchup – 2 tbsp.
- Brown sugar – 1 tbsp.
- Garlic cloves – 2, minced
- Onion – 1/2, minced

Method

1. Preheat the oven to broil.
2. Press salute on your pressure cooker.
3. Add oil and sauté the onion and garlic.
4. Then add the lemon juice, sugar, ketchup, and soy sauce. Mix well.
5. Add the ribs into the pot.
6. Press Chicken/Meat and cook for 35 minutes on Manual setting.
7. Do a quick release.
8. Remove the ribs and place on a baking sheet.
9. Broil them for 5 to 10 minutes in the oven.
10. Press sauté on the pot and thicken the sauce.
11. Serve with the sauce.

Nutritional Facts Per Serving

- Calories: 228
- Fat: 6.9g
- Carb: 14.9g
- Protein: 25.7g

Kare Kare is a traditional Pilipino dish. Traditionally it is cooked in a pressure cooker, but it is possible to cook the dish in the Instant Pot.

Pilipino Kare Kare

Cook time: 50 minutes	Servings: 2

Ingredients

- Oxtail – 150 grams
- Stew meat – 150 grams
- Water – 1 cup

- Onion – ½, sliced in wedges
- Peanut butter – 1 tbsp.
- Green beans – 1 tbsp.
- Eggplant – 100 grams, sliced
- Bok Choy – 1, prepared and cut in half
- Madrecita chicken seasoning – 1 tsp.
- Fish sauce – 1 tsp.

Method

1. Place the oxtail in the pot and add water and stew meat.
2. Close and press Meat. Cook on High pressure for 35 minutes.
3. Release pressure when cooked and open.
4. Remove the meat and oxtail and set aside.
5. If you want, you can refrigerate the broth overnight and skim off the fat.
6. Press sauté and heat the broth.
7. Add the sliced onion when the broth starts to boil.
8. Add the peanut butter after 1 minute. Continue to stir.
9. Add back the meat and oxtail and add the remaining ingredients.
10. Add the beans, bottom stalks of the bok choy, and eggplant after 2 minutes.
11. Add the chicken seasoning, fish sauce and stir to mix.
12. Top the dish with Bok Choy leaves. Gently press and cook for a few minutes.
13. Turn off the heat and serve.

Nutritional Facts Per Serving

- Calories: 211

- Fat: 9.9g
- Carb: 9.7g
- Protein: 21.8g

In the Philippines, people love to eat rice. This is a finger licking good, breakfast dish.

Filipino Beef Tapa

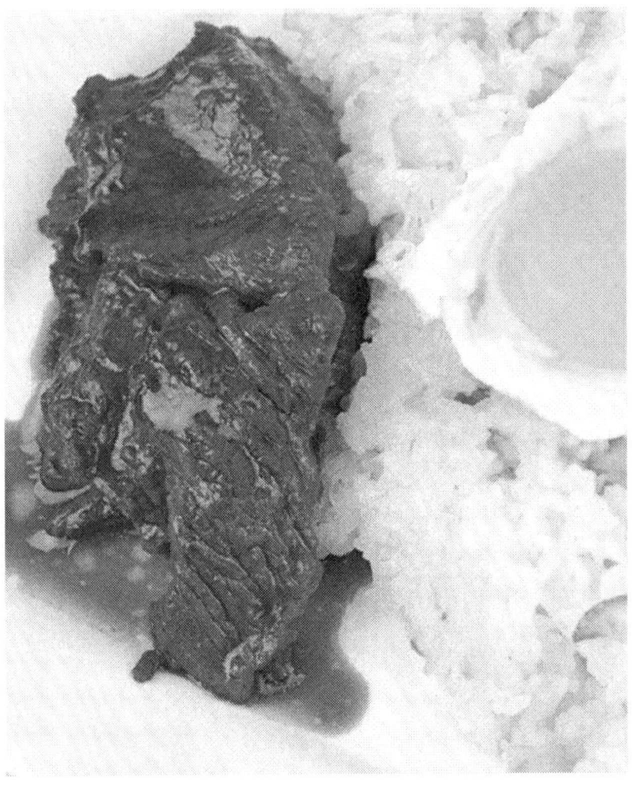

Cook time: 22 minutes	Servings: 2

Ingredients

- Beef sirloin – 1 lb. thin sliced
- Oil – 1 ½ tbsps.
- Minced garlic – 3 cloves

- Water – 1 cup
- Soy sauce – 1/3 cup
- Salt and pepper to taste
- Brown sugar – 1 ½ tbsp.
- Oyster sauce – ½ tbsp.
- Half lime – juiced
- Cornstarch – ½ tsp.
- Water – 1 tbsp.

Method

1. Press sauté on your pressure cooker.
2. Add the oil and garlic and cook for 2 minutes.
3. Add sliced sirloin and cook until both sides are brown.
4. Then add the oyster sauce, lime juice, water, soy sauce, salt, pepper, and brown sugar. Mix well.
5. Cover and cook on Manual High for 12 minutes.
6. Do a quick release and open the lid.
7. Mix cornstarch with water and add to the pot.
8. Turn on Sauté and let boil for 5 to 10 minutes. Continue to stir.
9. Remove from heat and serve.

Nutritional Facts Per Serving

- Calories: 320
- Fat: 17.7g
- Carb: 13.4g
- Protein: 26.5g

This short rib rice is tender and delicious. The sticky sauce makes it a favorite meal for most Koreans.

Korean Short Ribs

Korean Short Ribs

Cook time: 55 minutes	Servings: 2

Ingredients

- Bone-in beef short ribs – 500 grams
- Carrots – 80 grams, chopped
- Korean radish – 66 grams, chopped

Sauce

- Water – 3 tbsps.
- Red apple – 1/3, chopped
- Onion – 1/3, chopped
- Soy sauce – 2 tbsp.
- Brown sugar – ½ tbsp.
- Honey – ½ tbsp.
- Rice wine – ½ tbsp.
- Minced garlic – 1/3 tbsp.
- Sesame oil – ½ tsp.
- Whole black peppercorns - 1

Method

1. Boil the short ribs in boiling water for 6 to 8 minutes. Then drain and rinse in cold water. Place in the Instant Pot.
2. Blend the sauce ingredients in a mixer until smooth.
3. Pour sauce over the short ribs.
4. Cover with the lid and cook on High for 35 minutes.
5. Do a quick release and remove the lid.
6. Transfer the meat to a bowl, cover and set aside.
7. Add the vegetables into the pot.
8. Press Sauté and cook for 20 minutes.
9. Garnish with toasted sesame seeds.
10. Serve the ribs.

Nutritional Facts Per Serving

- Calories: 448
- Fat: 15.6g
- Carb: 22.7g
- Protein: 52.1g

CHAPTER 6 FISH AND SEAFOOD RECIPES

Rice porridge or Vietnamese fish congee is so flavorful and comforting. This delicious fish bowl will be cooked in 25 minutes .

Vietnamese Fish Congee (Chao ca)

Cook time: 25 minutes	Servings: 2

Ingredients

- Short grain white rice – 0.38 cup, Washed and drained
- Mung bean – 1 tbsp. Washed and drained
- Fish bones – 0.75 lb. scrub with salt and rinse in cold water
- Ginger – 1, thumb-sized piece, chopped
- Shallot – 0.5, chopped
- Water – 3 cups
- Salt – 0.5 tsp.
- Fish sauce – 0.5 tbsp.
- Fish fillet – 0.5 lb. sliced diagonal into ½ inch thick pieces

For toppings and herbs

- Black pepper
- Vietnamese perilla, sliced
- Chopped cilantro
- Sliced scallion
- Fried shallot

Method

1. Add the rice and bean to the Instant Pot.
2. Add the fish bones, sliced ginger, and chopped shallot.
3. Add fish sauce, salt, and water.
4. Cook on porridge mode for 20 minutes.
5. Season the fish fillets with salt and pepper. Set aside.
6. Release the pressure once cooked. Open, remove and discard fish bones.
7. Add fish fillets and cook on sauté for a couple of minutes or until fish is cooked.

8. Adjust seasoning.
9. Serve topped with herbs of your choice.

Nutritional Facts Per Serving

- Calories: 419
- Fat: 14.5g
- Carb: 52.6g
- Protein: 20.3g

This is a Vietnamese Salmon dish cooked in an Instant Pot. The fish is served with a Vietnamese sauce. The salmon is perfect served with rice.

Vietnamese Salmon

Cook time: 15 minutes	Servings: 2

Ingredients

- Olive oil – ½ tbsp.
- Light brown sugar – 2 tbsps.
- Asian fish sauce – 1 ½ tbsp.
- Soy sauce – ¾ tbsp.
- Grated fresh ginger – ¼ tsp.
- Finely grated zest of 1 lime
- Juice of ½ lime
- Freshly ground black pepper – ¼ tsp.

- Skinless salmon fillets – 2

For garnish:

- Fresh lime wedges
- Fresh cilantro leaves
- Sliced green onion

Method

1. Press Sauté on your Instant Pot.
2. Add oil, ginger, black pepper, lime juice, lime zest, soy sauce, fish sauce, and brown sugar to the IP. Bring to a simmer, then turn off the cooker.
3. Place the fish (keep the skin side up) into the cooker. Use a spoon to drop some sauce over the fish.
4. Cover and cook on Low for 1 minute. Do a natural release for 5 minutes.
5. Press Sauté and cook the fish for 30 seconds to 1 minute or until the fish is cooked.
6. Remove the fish and reduce the sauce until thickens, about 3 minutes.
7. Arrange the fish and sauce in serving bowls.
8. Garnish with cilantro leaves, sliced green onion, and fresh lime wedges.

Nutritional Facts Per Serving

- Calories: 225
- Fat: 6.5g
- Carb: 15.3g
- Protein: 27.7g

This is an Indian cooker shrimp curry dish. It is made in just 20 minutes. This dish is made with tomatoes, onions, garlic, ginger, and flavorful spices.

Indian Coconut Shrimp Curry

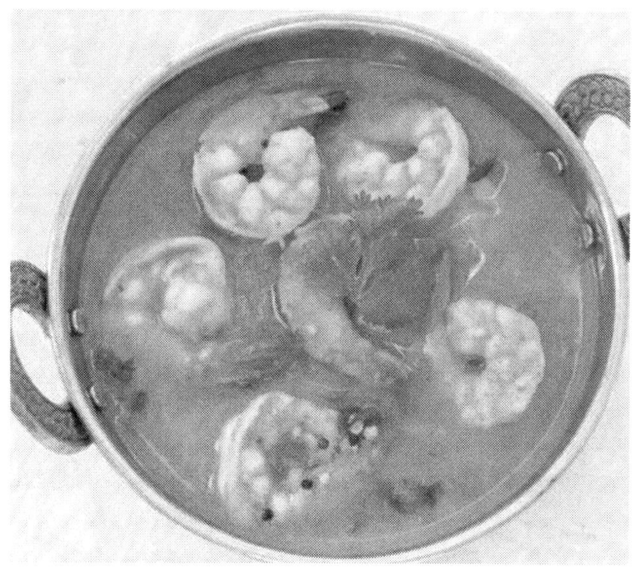

Cook time: 20 minutes	Servings: 2

Ingredients

- Shrimp, deveined tail-on – ½ lb.
- Oil – ½ tbsp.
- Mustard seeds – ½ tsp.
- Green chili pepper – 1, sliced
- Onion – ½ cup, chopped
- Ginger – 1 tsp. minced
- Garlic – 1 tsp. minced

- Tomato – ½ cup, chopped
- Coconut milk – 4 oz.
- Lime juice – ½ tbsp.
- Cilantro – 1 tsp.

Spices

- Ground turmeric – ¼ tsp.
- Cayenne – ½ tsp.
- Garam masala – ¼ tsp.
- Coriander powder – ½ tsp.
- Salt – ¼ tsp.

Method

1. Press the Sauté on your Instant Pot and add oil and mustard seeds.
2. Sizzle for a few seconds, then add the garlic, ginger, onions, and green chili.
3. Stir-fry until onions are golden brown, about 5 minutes.
4. Add the spices and tomato and mix. Stir-fry for 3 minutes.
5. Add the shrimp and coconut milk to the pot. Stir and press cancel.
6. Close the lid and press Manual.
7. Cook on low pressure for 3 minutes.
8. Do a natural release and open the lid.
9. Stir in lime juice and garnish with cilantro.
10. Enjoy with rice.

Nutritional Facts Per Serving

- Calories: 226
- Fat: 10g

- Carb: 8g
- Protein: 24g

Perfectly cooked moist and juice Instant Pot salmon. This succulent salmon is cooked in sweet-savory, caramelized teriyaki sauce.

Salmon (Singaporean)

Cook time: 5 minutes	Servings: 2

Ingredients

- Salmon steaks – 2, 1 to 1.5 inch thick
- Garlic – 4 cloves, crushed
- Ginger – 1 to 2 slices

Method

1. Soy sauce – ¼ cup

2. Mirin – ¼ cup
3. Japanese cooking sake – ¼ cup
4. Sesame oil – ¼ tsp.
5. White sugar – 2 tbsps.

Garnish

- Toasted sesame seeds
- Green onion – 1 stalk, sliced

Thickener

- Cornstarch – 2 ½ tbsps.
- Water – 3 tbsps.

Method

1. In the Instant Pot, add ginger and garlic.
2. Layer salmon steaks on the garlic cloves.
3. To make the sauce: mix the sauce ingredients and pour over salmon.
4. Pressure cook at High for 0 (zero) minute and do a natural release for 10 minutes.
5. Check the fish with a food thermometer (around 145F).
6. Place the salmon on serving plates.
7. Thicken the sauce over Sauté button.
8. Serve.

Nutritional Facts Per Serving

- Calories: 657
- Fat: 20g
- Carb: 39g
- Protein: 67g

This salmon dish is cooked with ginger, lime, and Asian fish sauce. The fish cooks very quickly and is wonderfully tender.

Vietnamese Caramel Salmon

Cook time: 10 minutes	Servings: 2

Ingredients

- Olive oil – ½ tbsp.
- Light brown sugar – 2 tbsps.
- Asian fish sauce – 1 ½ tbsps.
- Soy sauce – ¾ tbsp.
- Grated fresh ginger – ½ tsp.
- Zest of half a lime
- Juice of ½ lime
- Black pepper to taste

- Salmon fillets – 2, skinless (6 to 8 ounces each)
- Fresh cilantro and sliced scallions for garnish

Method

1. Press Sauté on your pressure cooker.
2. Add the oil, sugar, soy sauce, fish sauce, ginger, black pepper, lime zest, and juice in the pressure cooker and whisk to mix.
3. Bring to a simmer and turn off the heat.
4. Place the fish in the pressure cooker.
5. Spoon the sauce over the fish.
6. Cover and cook on Low for 1 minute.
7. Do a natural release for 5 minutes.
8. Remove the fish.
9. Press sauté and thicken the sauce for 3 minutes.
10. Spoon the sauce over the fish.
11. Garnish with cilantro and scallions.
12. Serve.

Nutritional Facts Per Serving

- Calories: 399
- Fat: 23g
- Carb: 19.3g
- Protein: 29.5g

This healthy Asian Salmon dish is delicious and free from gluten and soy.

Soy-Free Asian Salmon

Cook time: 10 minutes	Servings: 2

Ingredients

- Salmon fillets – 2 (6 oz.)
- Coconut oil – 1 tbsp.

- Brown sugar – 1 tbsp.
- Coconut aminos – 3 tbsps.
- Maple syrup – 2 tbsps.
- Paprika - 1 tsp.
- Ginger – ¼ tsp.
- Sesame seeds – 1 tsp.
- Fresh scallions

Method

1. Press sauté on your IP.
2. Add oil and brown sugar. Stir and melt the sugar.
3. Add the aminos, ginger, paprika, and maple. Mix.
4. Add the salmon, skin side up.
5. Season with salt and pepper.
6. Cover and cook on Low for 2 minutes.
7. Do a natural release for 5 minutes.
8. Serve garnished with parsley and sesame seeds.

Nutritional Facts Per Serving

- Calories: 438
- Fat: 25.9g
- Carb: 11g
- Protein: 40.2g

This Chinese Steamed fish recipe is high protein, low-carb, gluten-free and paleo.

Ginger Scallion Fish

Cook time: 10 minutes	Servings: 2

Ingredients

Mix and marinate

- Soy sauce – 1 ½ tbsps.
- Rice wine – 1 tbsp.
- Chicken black bean paste – ½ tbsp.
- Minced ginger – ½ tsp.
- Garlic – ½ tsp.
- Firm white fish – ½ pound

Vegetables

- Peanut oil – ½ tbsp.
- Julienned ginger – 1 tbsp.
- Julienned green onion – 2 tbsps.
- Chopped cilantro – 2 tbsps.
- Water – 1 cup

Method

1. Place fish pieces on a plate.
2. Mix the ingredients for the sauce in a bowl.
3. Pour over the fish and marinate for 30 minutes.
4. Meanwhile, chop the vegetables and set aside.
5. Add 1 cup water in the IP and add a steamer.
6. Remove the fish from the marinade. Reserve the marinade.
7. Place the fish in the steamer basket.
8. Cook the fish on Low for 2 minutes.
9. Do a quick release.
10. Heat a saucepan.
11. Add oil and add ginger in the hot oil.
12. Sauté for 10 seconds, then add the cilantro and scallions.
13. Stir fry for 2 minutes and add the reserved marinade.
14. Allow to boil until cooked through.
15. Pour over the fish and serve.

Nutritional Facts Per Serving

- Calories: 171
- Fat: 5g
- Carb: 4g

- Protein: 24g

This delicious Instant Pot Indian fish biryani is made with brown basmati rice.

Fish Biryani

Cook time: 30 minutes	Servings: 2

Ingredients

- Butter – ¾ tbsp.
- Onion – ¼, chopped
- Grated ginger – ¼ tsp.
- Brown basmati rice – ¾ cup, rinsed and dried

- Water – ½ cup
- Thin coconut milk – ¼ cup
- Salt – ¼ tsp.
- Roma tomatoes – ¾, chopped

Fish and marinades

- Boneless, skinless firm white fish fillet – ½ lb. cut into large chunk
- Turmeric – a pinch
- Chili powder - 1/2 tsp.
- Salt to taste

Spices

- Bay leaves – 1
- Cinnamon stick – ¼
- Clove – 1
- Turmeric – 1 pinch
- Cardamom pod – 1
- Coriander powder – a pinch
- Garam masala – a pinch

Fresh herbs

- Mint leaves and cilantro leaves

Method

1. Marinade the fish in marinade ingredients for 20 minutes.
2. Press sauté on your Instant Pot and add butter.
3. Add onion and stir fry until soft.
4. Add ginger and all the spice ingredients and sauté until fragrant.
5. Add the fish and gently mix.

6. Cook until cooked through, 2 minutes, remove the fish and turn off the sauté mode
7. Pour in liquid and salt. Deglaze the pot.
8. Add mint leaves, cilantro, and tomatoes.
9. Sprinkle the rice on top. Make sure the rice is covered by liquid.
10. Cover and cook on High pressure for 20 minutes.
11. Do a natural release.
12. Open the lid and gently fluff the rice.
13. Place the cooked fish pieces into the pot.
14. Garnish with cilantro leaves and serve.

Nutritional Facts Per Serving

- Calories: 477
- Fat: 15.8g
- Carb: 55.4g
- Protein: 24.5g

This Southeast Asian fish dish is spicy, coconutty and filling.

Pressure Cooked Coconut Fish Curry

Cook time: 10 minutes	Servings: 2

Ingredients

- Fish fillets or steaks – ½ lb. cut into bite size pieces
- Tomato – ½, chopped
- Green chilies – 1, sliced
- Onion – ½, chopped
- Garlic – 1 clove, minced
- Grated ginger – 1 tsp.
- Curry leaves – 2
- Ground coriander – ½ tsp.
- Ground turmeric – 1 pinch

- Chili powder – a pinch
- Ground fenugreek a pinch
- Unsweetened coconut milk – ½ cup
- Salt to taste
- Lemon juice to taste

Method

1. Preheat the pressure cooker.
2. Add oil and drop the curry leaves.
3. Fry for 1 minutc.
4. Add the ginger, garlic, and onion and sauté until onion is soft.
5. Add all the ground spiced and sauté for 2 minutes.
6. Deglaze the pot with coconut milk.
7. Add fish pieces, tomato, and green chili. Mix.
8. Cover and cook on 5 minutes on Low.
9. Do a natural release.
10. Add salt, and lemon juice before serving.
11. Serve.

Nutritional Facts Per Serving

- Calories: 160
- Fat: 4.1g
- Carb: 5.3g
- Protein: 23.6g

This steamed black cod only take 2 minutes and cooks perfectly in the Instant Pot.

Chinese Steamed Black Cod

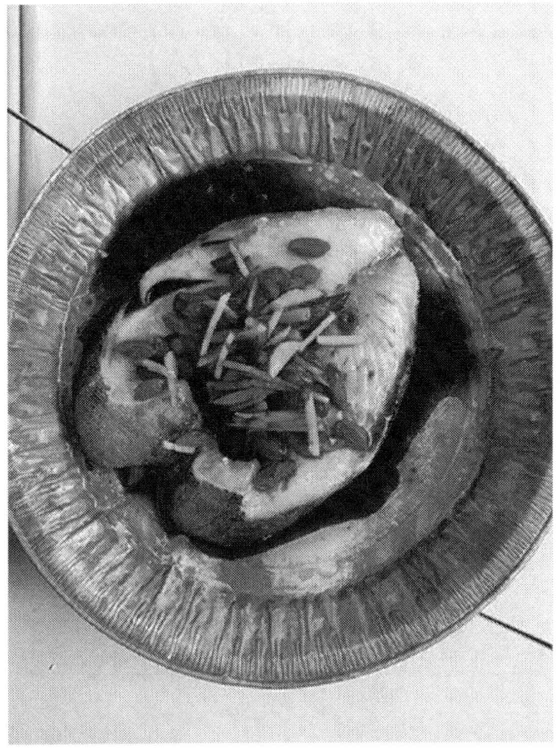

Cook time: 10 minutes	Servings: 2

Ingredients

- Black cod fillet – 2
- Ginger – 2 tsps. minced (divided)
- Goji berries to taste
- Water – 1 cup

Sauce

- Soy cause – 2 tbsps.
- Sugar – 1 tsp.
- Canola oil – ½ tbsp.

Method

1. Add 1 cup water to the IP.
2. In a dish, place the fish.
3. Top with goji berries, and ginger slices.
4. Place a steamer rack in the IP.
5. Place the dish with the fish on top of the steamer rack.
6. Cover and press steam.
7. Cook on Low for 2 minutes.
8. Mix in sugar and soy sauce. Taste and adjust accordingly.
9. Once cooked, do a natural release.
10. Open the lid and remove the fish.
11. Heat oil in a pan over the stove. Turn heat off.
12. Place the remaining ginger slices on the fish.
13. Pour with hot oil.
14. Add sugar and soy mixture to the hot pan on the stove.
15. Let it bubble, but don't burn.
16. Pour sizzling sugar-soy mixture over the fish.
17. Serve.

Nutritional Facts Per Serving

- Calories: 246
- Fat: 4.4g
- Carb: 15.8g
- Protein: 20.3g

CHAPTER 7 RICE RECIPES

This rice dish is made with sweet rice and features mushrooms, chicken, and sausage. For many Chinese, this dish is a favorite lunch meal.

Chinese Sticky Rice

Cook time: 12 minutes	Servings: 2

Ingredients for chicken

- Skinless, boneless chicken thighs – 3 ounces, cut into pieces
- Soy sauce – ½ tsp.
- Rice wine – ½ tsp.
- Sesame oil – ½ tsp.
- Salt and black pepper to taste

Sticky Rice

- Oil – 1 tsp.
- Chopped scallion – 1
- Ginger – 1 tsp. minced
- Short grain sweet rice – ½ cup, rinsed 4 to 5 times, drained
- Chinese sausage – 1 link, chopped
- Dried shitake mushrooms – 2, chopped (soak them in hot water for 30 minutes then, reserve the liquid)
- Dried shrimp - 1 tbsp. (soak them in hot water and reserve the liquid)
- Chicken broth – ½ cup, mixed with reserved liquids
- Soy sauce – 1 tsp.
- Rice wine – 1 tsp.
- Sesame oil – ½ tsp.
- Pepper to taste

Method

1. Mix chicken pieces with sesame oil, rice wine, soy sauce, salt, and pepper. Set aside.
2. Press sauté on your Instant Pot.
3. Add oil and add ginger and scallion in the hot Instant Pot.

4. Sauté until fragrant.
5. Add marinated chicken and sauté until lightly browned.
6. Add shrimp, mushrooms, sausage, and sweet rice.
7. Sauté a few minutes. Stir a few times.
8. Add the broth and liquid mixture, sesame oil, rice wine, soy sauce, and pepper.
9. Press Cancel and press Rice. Cook for 12 minutes.
10. Release pressure and serve.

Nutritional Facts Per Serving

- Calories: 302
- Fat: 5g
- Carb: 41g
- Protein: 17g

This is a Japanese rice dish made with azuki beans and glutinous rice. Japanese eat this dish as a part of the New Year celebration.

Sekihan – Azuki Bean Rice (Japanese)

Cook time: 40 minutes	Servings: 2

Ingredients

- Glutinous rice - 2/3 cup

- Azuki beans – 2 tbsp.
- Water – ¾ cup
- Salt – 1/3 tsp.
- Black sesame to sprinkle

Method

1. Wash the beans and drain.
2. Add the beans and water in the Instant Pot.
3. Close the lid and cook on low pressure for 10 minutes.
4. Meanwhile, wash the rice and drain.
5. Do a quick release when cooked.
6. Open the lid and add the rice and season with salt.
7. Close the lid and cook on low for 3 minutes more.
8. When finished cooking, do a natural release.
9. Serve sprinkled with black sesame.

Nutritional Facts Per Serving

- Calories: 240
- Fat: 1g
- Carb: 52g
- Protein: 4g

This Indian rice dish is tangy, light and refreshing. You can eat it as a meal or a side dish. Add pickles or yogurt when eating.

Indian Lemon Rice

Cook time: 20 minutes	Servings: 2

Ingredients

- Basmati rice – ½ cup, soaked for 30 minutes and rinsed
- Olive oil – 1 ½ tbsp.
- Black mustard seeds – ½ tsp.
- Split chickpeas – ½ tbsp.
- Split and skinless black lentils – 1/2 tbsp.
- Raw peanuts – 2 tbsp.
- Curry leaves – 5
- Green chili – 1, sliced
- Minced ginger – ½ tsp.

- Salt – ½ tsp.
- Coriander powder – ½ tsp.
- Turmeric – 1 pinch
- Lemon juice – 1 tbsp.
- Lemon zest – 1 tsp.
- Water – 1 cup

Method

1. Press the sauté button on the IP and add the oil.
2. Add the black lentils, chickpeas and mustard seeds in the hot oil. Stir-fry for 2 minutes. Add the raw peanuts and stir-fry for 2 minutes.
3. Add the salt, turmeric, coriander, ginger, green chilies, and curry leaves and stir-fry for 30 seconds.
4. Add the rice, water, lemon juice, and zest. Mix well.
5. Cover with the lid and cook on high pressure for 6 minutes.
6. Do a natural release for 10 minutes.
7. Fluff the rice with a fork and serve.

Nutritional Facts Per Serving

- Calories: 332
- Fat: 8g
- Carb: 55g
- Protein: 7g

This is Indonesian fried rice, known as Nasi Goreng. Made with brown rice, this healthy and flavorful dish is made quickly using Instant Pot.

Indonesian Fried Rice (Nasi Goreng)

Cook time: 22 minutes	Servings: 2

Ingredients

- Oil – 1 ½ tbsps.
- Onion – ½, chopped
- Minced garlic – ½ tbsp.
- Fresh chilies – 1, minced
- Boneless, skinless chicken thighs – 1, cut into small pieces

- Carrots – 1, chopped
- Beet – ½, chopped
- Chopped mushrooms – 2 tbsp.
- Brown basmati rice – ½ cup
- Kecap Manis – ½ tbsp. sweet soy sauce
- Tamari or fish sauce – ½ tbsp.
- Tamarind paste – ½ tsp.
- Water – ½ cup

To garnish

- Chopped scallions
- Lime wedges
- Chopped cilantro
- 1 egg per person

Method

1. Press the sauté and add the oil. Heat it for 1 minute.
2. Add in the onions and sauté for 3 minutes.
3. Add in the chili and garlic and sauté for 1 more minute.
4. Add the vegetables and chicken and mix well.
5. Add the rice and mix well.
6. Add the tamari, tamarind, soy sauce, and ½ cup water.
7. Cancel sauté. Cook on high for 7 minutes.
8. Then do a natural release for 10 minutes.
9. Open and mix well.
10. Crack the eggs on top of the rice.
11. Cover so the eggs get cooked via steam.
12. Serve garnished with lime, cilantro, and scallions.

Nutritional Facts Per Serving

- Calories: 328
- Fat: 15.7g
- Carb: 37.7g
- Protein: 10.1g

This easy recipe is comfort food for many Singaporeans. The chicken is tender and moist, and the sauce has spicy, sweet and savory flavors.

Hainanese Chicken Rice in Pressure Cooker (Singaporean)

Cook time: 40 minutes	Servings: 2

Ingredients

Chicken

- Whole chicken legs – 2
- Green onions – 3 stalks, cut into 2 inches long
- Shallot – 1, roughly minced

- Garlic - 6 cloves, roughly minced
- Ginger – 2 tbsps. sliced
- Unsalted chicken stock - 1 ½ cups
- Sea salt – 1 tbsp.
- Olive oil – 1 tbsp.

Rice

- Jasmine rice – 1 cup
- Chicken stock from the pot – ½ cup
- Water – ½ cup
- Olive oil – 1 tbsp.
- Garlic – 2 cloves, minced

Chicken stock soup

- Remaining chicken stock
- Water
- Lettuce or cabbage
- Chopped green onions for garnish

Sweet soy sauce

- Dark soy sauce – 1 tbsp.
- Shaoxing wine – 1 tbsp.
- Chicken stock – ½ tbsp. from the pot
- Sugar – 1 tsp.
- Sesame oil – 2 drops

Green onion ginger sauce

- Green onions – 1 stalk, finely chopped
- Ginger – 1 tbsp. grated
- Peanut oil – 1 ½ tbsps. heated
- Salt to taste

Chicken chili sauce

- Hot sauce – 2 tbsps.
- Ginger – 2 tbsps. grated
- Garlic – 3 cloves, minced
- Lime – 1 juiced
- Chicken stock – 1 tsp. from the pot

Method

1. Press Sauté and heat up the pressure cooker.
2. Add oil and sauté the garlic, ginger, shallot, and green onions for 2 minutes.
3. Add 1 ½ cups of chicken stock and deglaze the pot. Add salt and mix well.
4. Place the chicken legs into the pot.
5. Close and cook on High pressure for 8 minutes.
6. Do a natural release for 10 minutes.
7. Open the lid and remove the chicken legs from the pot.
8. Cool the chicken in cold water, then place on a cooling rack.
9. Strain the chicken stock.
10. Mix ½-cup water and ½ cup of chicken stock together. Don't make it too salty.
11. To make the rice: Clean the pressure cooker and add 1 tbsp. olive oil.
12. Sauté garlic and add 1 cup of jasmine rice, and 1-cup water-stock mixture.
13. Close lid and cook at High pressure for 3 minutes.
14. Do a natural release.
15. For the ginger sauce: place all the ingredients in a bowl and mix well.
16. To make the soy sauce: mix all the ingredients together.
17. Prepare the chicken chili sauce: mix all the ingredients.
18. Prepare the chicken soup: in a pan, heat the chicken stock and add water if it is too salty.
19. Add cabbage and cook for 1 minute
20. Garnish with chopped onions and serve on the side.

Nutritional Facts Per Serving

- Calories: 859
- Fat: 51.9g
- Carb: 35.5g

- Protein: 60.3g

This is a delicious and easy Instant Pot Chinese fried rice recipe.

Fried Rice

Cook time: 43 minutes	Servings: 2

Ingredients

- Jasmin rice – 1 cup
- Cold water – 2 cups
- Salt to taste
- Peanut oil – 1 tbsp. plus 1 tsp.
- Eggs – 2 mixed with rice, 2 scrambled
- Frozen vegetables – ½ cup, thawed
- Green onions – 1 stalk, sliced
- A dash of white pepper

Method

1. Add 1 tbsp. peanut oil, and rice in a bowl. Mix well.
2. Add enough water in the bowl and make sure the rice is submerged.
3. Add 1 cup water in the Instant Pot and steamer rack.
4. Layer the rice bowl on the rack.
5. Cook at High for 8 minutes, then do a 10-minute natural release.
6. Meanwhile, prepare the eggs and sliced green onions.
7. Beat the eggs and separate in two bowls.
8. Mix the very hot rice with 2 beaten eggs. Mix well.
9. Discard the hot water and dry.
10. Cook the remaining two eggs in the Instant Pot on Sauté setting with oil. Scramble the eggs and set aside.
11. Add the remaining oil.
12. Add egg mixed rice in the Instant Pot.
13. Wait 1 minute and give it a quick stir.
14. Repeat step 13, for 5 times.
15. Add the vegetables and mix well.
16. Sprinkle with salt and pepper and add the scrambled eggs.
17. Mix well.
18. Add in the sliced green onions and mix well.

Nutritional Facts Per Serving

- Calories: 381
- Fat: 13g
- Carb: 53g
- Protein: 10g

Also known as forbidden rice, this black rice is a superfood. The rice is nutrient-packed and high in antioxidant.

Black Rice

Cook time: 34 minutes	Servings: 2

Ingredients

- Black rice – 1 cup, washed and rinsed
- Water – 1 cup

Method

1. Add the rice and water in the inner pot.
2. Cover and pressure cook at High pressure for 18 minutes, then do a natural release for 10 minutes.

3. Open the lid, fluff and serve.

Nutritional Facts Per Serving

- Calories: 397
- Fat: 3g
- Carb: 83g
- Protein: 8g

This recipe is cooked with raw white Jasmine rice. You can cook it in a pressure cooker or Instant Pot in under 15 minutes.

Chinese Fried Rice

Cook time: 5 minutes	Servings: 2

Ingredients

- Jasmine rice – 2/3 cup
- Peanut oil – ½ tbsp. divided
- Onion – 2 tbsps. diced
- Fresh garlic – 1/3 tbsp. minced

- Freshwater or broth – 4 oz.
- Soy sauce – ½ tbsp.
- Carrot – 1, finely chopped
- Frozen peas and or corn – ½ cup

After pressure release

- Egg – 1
- Cabbage – 1/3 cup, chopped
- Scallions – 1, chopped
- Bean sprouts – 1/3 cup
- Toasted sesame oil – 1/3 tsp.

Method

1. Press Sauté on your pressure cooker and heat.
2. Add oil and diced onions.
3. Stir fry for 3 minutes.
4. Add rice and toast for 2 minutes.
5. Add garlic and toast for 15 seconds more.
6. Add water and soy sauce and deglaze the cooking pot.
7. Mix in corn, peas, and carrots.
8. Cover and cook on High pressure for 1 minute.
9. Do a natural release.
10. Whisk the egg in a small bowl and set aside.
11. Remove lid and press Sauté.
12. Push rice to one side of the pot.
13. Add the rest of the peanut oil and pour in half of the whisked egg.
14. Scramble until soft and then mix into the rice.
15. Pour the rest of the whisked eggs over the rice and mix well.
16. Add bean sprouts, scallions, and cabbage.
17. Mix until cabbage has wilted.

18. Drizzle sesame oil over rice and serve.

Nutritional Facts Per Serving

- Calories: 361
- Fat: 7g
- Carb: 59g
- Protein: 12g

This rich Congee dish is simple with 6 ingredients and 6 steps.

Chinese Chicken Congee

Cook time: 30 minutes	Servings: 2

Ingredients

- Jasmine rice – 1/3 cup, rinsed and drained
- Cold water – 2 1/3 cup
- Chicken drumsticks – 2
- Ginger – 1 tsp. sliced
- Green onion for garnish

- Salt to taste

Method

1. Add water, rice, ginger, and chicken into the IP.
2. Close the lid and cook on High for 30 minutes.
3. Do a natural release.
4. Open the lid and press sauté.
5. Stir and sauté until thickens.
6. Season with salt
7. Remove the bones from the meat and remove the skin and bone.
8. Garnish and serve.

Nutritional Facts Per Serving

- Calories: 138
- Fat: 2.3g
- Carb: 16g
- Protein: 12.2g

This dish is known as Kabocha Squash. This Japanese pumpkin rice dish is easy to make and delicious.

Japanese Pumpkin Rice

Cook time: 10 minutes	Servings: 2

Ingredients

- Japanese pumpkin – 2 cups, cubed
- Japanese short grain rice – 1 ½ cups, rinsed
- Cold water – 1 ½ cups

- Japanese cooking sake – 1 tbsp.
- Sea salt – 1 tsp.
- Sesame oil – 4 drops

Method

1. Add the sake, water, rice, sea salt, and sesame oil in the IP.
2. Mix and add squash.
3. Close the lid and cook at High for 7 minutes.
4. Do a natural release.
5. Remove the lid.
6. Mix and serve.

Nutritional Facts Per Serving

- Calories: 341
- Fat: 3g
- Carb: 76g
- Protein: 6g

CHAPTER 8 SIDE-DISHES RECIPES

This recipe uses chicken, vegetables, and broth and makes a flavorful, healthy, and delicious Chinese chicken soup within only 30 minutes.

Chinese Chicken Soup

Cook time: 40 minutes	Servings: 2

Ingredients for broth

- Bone-in, skin-on chicken thighs – 2
- Chicken stock – 1 cup
- Ginger – 1 slice
- Green onions- 2, chopped

Soup

- Carrots – 2, sliced
- Zucchinis – 1, sliced
- Mushrooms – ½ pound, sliced
- Salt and black pepper to taste

Method

1. In the Instant Pot, combine green onion, ginger, water, chicken stock, and chicken.
2. Press manual and set the timer for 30 minutes.
3. When cooked, remove ginger and green onion from the soup and discard.
4. Add mushroom, zucchini, and carrot to the soup.
5. Cover and sauté until vegetables are cooked through.
6. Adjust the seasoning and serve.

Nutritional Facts Per Serving

- Calories: 192
- Fat: 3.4g
- Carb: 15.1g
- Protein: 27.1g

This Indo-Chinese soup is perfect for the winter season or during a rainy day. This soup is very similar to the restaurant style sweet corn soup.

Sweet Corn Soup

Cook time: 20 minutes	Servings: 2

Ingredients

- Sweet corn – 1 1/3 cups, divided
- Water – ½ cup
- Oil – ½ tbsp.
- Ginger – 1 tsp. minced
- Garlic – 1 tsp. minced
- Carrots – ½ cup, diced
- Spring onions – 2 ½ stalks, chopped, green and white parts separated

- Vegetable broth – 1 2/3 cups
- Salt to taste
- Black pepper to taste
- Sugar – 1/3 tsp.
- Vinegar – 2/3 tsp.
- Cornstarch – 2 tsps. mixed with ¼ cup water
- Red chili paste to taste

Method

1. Blend ¾ cup sweet corn and ½ cup water in a blender to make a paste.
2. Press sauté on your Instant Pot.
3. Add oil to the hot pot and add garlic and ginger. Stir-fry for 30 seconds.
4. Add spring onion whites, carrots, sweet corn paste, and remaining corn.
5. Add the vinegar, sugar, salt, black pepper, and broth. Stir to mix well.
6. Press cancel and cover with the lid.
7. Press Manual and cook on High for 2 minutes.
8. Do a natural release for 10 minutes.
9. Add the water-cornstarch mixture and mix well.
10. Press sauté and let it come to a quick boil.
11. Use the green part of spring onions to garnish and add chili sauce to taste.
12. Serve.

Nutritional Facts Per Serving

- Calories: 181
- Fat: 6g

- Carb: 31g
- Protein: 4g

Monggo guisado or mug bean stew is a favorite dish. This dish can be cooked using shrimp or pork. If you are vegan, then omit both pork and shrimp.

Filipino Mung Bean Stew

Cook time: 15 minutes	Servings: 2

Ingredients

- Coconut oil – ½ tbsp.
- Garlic – 1 ½ cloves, minced
- Onion – 1/3, minced

- Pork – 1/3 lb. ground
- Mung beans – 2/3 cup, rinsed
- Water – 1 ½ cups
- Moringa leaves – 2/3 pack or spinach
- Sea salt to taste

Method

1. Press Sauté and melt the coconut oil in the Instant Pot.
2. Add onions and garlic and sauté until translucent.
3. Add pork and sauté until lightly browned.
4. Turn off the sauté.
5. Add the moringa leaves, water, and mung beans. If using spinach, then add at the end.
6. Cover and cook on Bean/Chili for 10 minutes.
7. Do a natural release.
8. Season with salt and serve.

Nutritional Facts Per Serving

- Calories: 375
- Fat: 9.3g
- Carb: 46.2g
- Protein: 27.9g

You can cook this tasty Filipino dish in the Instant Pot. Prepare for 5 minutes, cook for 25 minutes and your meal is ready!

Filipino Arroz Caldo

Cook time: 30 minutes	Servings: 2

Ingredients

- Olive oil or butter – 1 tbsp.
- Onion – ½, chopped
- Ginger – ½ inch, sliced
- Chicken thigh – 3 pieces, cut in half
- Uncooked rice – ½ cup
- Water – 4 cups
- Lemon – ½ lemon
- Fish sauce – 1 ½ tbsps.
- Salt – 1 tsp.
- Pepper – 1 tsp.

- Chopped green onion as a topping

Method

1. Press Sauté and add oil in the Instant Pot.
2. Add ginger and onion and sauté for 2 minutes.
3. Place chicken (skin side down) and sauté for 1 minute.
4. Add fish sauce, salt, pepper, lemon juice, rice, and water. Mix.
5. Cover and press Soup. Cook for 25 minutes on normal.
6. Once cooked, do a natural release.
7. Open and skim about ½ cup of the liquid from the top.
8. Serve.

Nutritional Facts Per Serving

- Calories: 423
- Fat: 10.1g
- Carb: 44g
- Protein: 36.7g

This Sri Lankan creamy spiced Dal Curry is easy to cook and delicious to eat. It is spiced with fenugreek seeds and cinnamon.

Sri Lankan Red Lentil Curry

Cook time: 30 minutes	Servings:2

Ingredients

- Red lentils – ¾ cup
- Fenugreek seeds – ¼ tsp.
- Black peppercorns – 1/3 tsp.
- Cayenne to taste
- Turmeric – ¼ tsp.
- Oil – 1 tsp.

- Mustard seeds – ½ tsp.
- Curry leaves – 6 to 8
- Small red onion – ½ chopped
- Cinnamon stick – 2 inches
- Water – 1 ½ cups
- Salt to taste
- Coconut milk – ¼ cup
- Tomato -1, chopped
- Lemon juice – ½ tsp.
- Shredded coconut – 1 tbsp.

Method

1. Wash and soak the red lentils.
2. Grind the black pepper, fenugreek, cayenne, turmeric into a powder and set aside
3. Press sauté on your Instant Pot.
4. Heat oil over medium heat.
5. Add mustard seeds, curry leaves and mix. add the powdered fenugreek seeds and cook and stir for 10 seconds.
6. Add salt, cinnamon, and onions. Mix to coat with spices. Cook for about 3 minutes.
7. Deglaze with a bit of water.
8. Add the lemon juice, half of the tomato, salt, water, milk, and lentils.
9. Close the lid and cook on high pressure for 3 minutes, then do a quick release after 5 minutes.
10. Fold in the rest of the tomatoes and lemon.
11. Test and adjust seasoning.
12. Add some shredded coconut and serve.

Nutritional Facts Per Serving

- Calories: 316
- Fat: 9g
- Carb: 43g
- Protein: 16g

Cooked sticky rice is wrapped in a delicate wrapper to make it a delicious side meal.

Shanghai Siu Mai (Chinese)

Cook time: 45 minutes	Servings: 10 dumplings

Ingredients

- Glutinous rice – 1/3 cup
- Chinese sausage – 2/3, diced
- Shitake mushrooms – 1, diced
- Liquid – ½ cup (from soaking mushrooms)

- Cooking oil – 2/3 tbsp.
- Shu Mai wrappers – 8

Aromatics

- Garlic – 2 cloves, chopped

Seasonings

- Sugar – 1/3 tsp.
- Soy sauce – ½ tsp.
- Oyster sauce – 1/3 tbsp.
- Dark soy sauce – 1/3 tsp.

Method

1. In a dish, add the sticky rice, aromatics, and seasonings, and the liquid + water into the sticky rice mixture. Make sure the rice is covered with water.
2. Set a trivet inside the Instant Pot.
3. Place the dish on top of the trivet and close the IP.
4. Cook on High for 30 minutes.
5. Then do a natural release.
6. Remove the bowl.
7. To wrap: place some sticky rice mixture on the middle of each wrapper and wrap nicely. Continue until you finish the filling.
8. Steam the wrapper on a high heat for 8 to 10 minutes.
9. Serve.

Nutritional Facts Per Dumpling

- Calories: 108
- Fat: 3.4g

- Carb: 17.2g
- Protein: 2.7g

Make this Chinese pork ribs bitter melon soup with Instant Pot.

Pork Ribs with Bitter Melon Soup

Cook time: 30 minutes	Servings: 2

Ingredients

- Pork ribs – ½ lb.
- Bitter melon – ½, prepared
- Salt – 1 tsp.
- Carrots – 1, chopped
- Water to cover

Seasonings

- Ground bean paste – 1 ½ tbsps.
- Soy sauce – 1 tbsp.
- Sugar – ½ tsp.

Aromatics

- Coriander – 1 bunch (stems for soup, leaves for garnish)
- Fried shallots – 2 tbsps.

Garnish

- Coriander leaves

Method

1. Put the carrot, bitter melon, and pork in the IP and add water to cover everything.
2. Add the seasonings and aromatics. Mix.
3. Close the lid.
4. Cook on High for 30 minutes, if the ribs are cut into bigger pieces.
5. Do a natural release.
6. Taste and adjust seasoning.
7. Garnish with chopped coriander and serve.

Nutritional Facts Per Serving

- Calories: 336
- Fat: 23.9g
- Carb: 15.9g
- Protein: 14.7g

This is an Indian healthy cauliflower and potato made in Instant Pot.

Cauliflower and Potato Stir Fry

Cook time: 15 minutes	Servings: 2

Ingredients

- Cauliflower – 2 cups, cut into florets
- Cubed potato – 1 cup
- Ghee – 1 tbsp.
- Cumin seeds – ½ tsp.
- Green chili pepper – 1, split into two
- Onion – ½, chopped
- Tomato – ½ chopped
- Ginger – 1 tsp. minced
- Garlic – 1 tsp. minced

- Dry mango powder – ½ tsp. or lemon juice
- Cilantro for garnish

Spices

- Ground turmeric – ¼ tsp.
- Red chili powder – ¼ tsp.
- Coriander powder – ½ tsp.
- Garam masala – ¼ tsp.
- Salt – ½ tsp.

Method

1. Press Sauté on your IP and heat oil.
2. Add green chili and cumin seeds, sauté for 30 seconds.
3. Add garlic paste, ginger, and diced onions. Stir them.
4. Add all the spices and chopped tomatoes.
5. Add potato cubes and mix.
6. Stir fry for 2 minutes.
7. Add cauliflower florets and mix.
8. Remove any stuck bits from the bottom.
9. Add 1/8 cup water and deglaze the pot if necessary.
10. Cover and press Manual.
11. Cook on Low for 2 minutes.
12. Do a natural release.
13. Add dry mango powder and garnish with cilantro.
14. Serve.

Nutritional Facts Per Serving

- Calories: 153
- Fat: 7.83g
- Carb: 19.42g
- Protein: 4.59g

This Indian egg curry is made by adding boiled eggs to a curry sauce. Curry sauce and the coconut milk make it a flavorful protein-rich dish.

Egg Curry

Cook time: 25 minutes	Servings: 2

Ingredients

- Eggs – 3
- Ghee – 1 tbsp.
- Cumin seeds – ½ tsp.
- Green chili – 1, sliced
- Onion – ¾ cup, chopped
- Ginger – 1 tsp, minced

- Garlic – 1 tsp, minced
- Tomato – ¾ cup, diced
- Water – ½ cup, divided
- Coconut milk – ¼ cup
- Lemon juice – ½ tbsp.
- Cilantro – 1 tbsp. for garnish

Spices

- Ground turmeric – ¼ tsp.
- Coriander powder – 1 tsp.
- Kashmiri red chili powder – ¼ tsp.
- Garam masala – ¼ tsp.
- Salt – ¼ tsp.

Whole spices

- Cinnamon – ½ stick
- Bay leaf – 1
- Black peppercorns – ½ tsp.
- Green cardamom – 1

Method

1. Press Sauté on your IP.
2. Add oil, cumin seeds, and whole spices.
3. Add garlic, ginger, onion, and green chili once the cumin changes color.
4. Stir fry for 3 minutes.
5. Add spices and tomato.
6. Stir fry for 2 minutes.
7. Add ¼ cup water and deglaze the pot.
8. Place the trivet, and a steel bowl with eggs in it.
9. Cover with the lid and cook on High for 6 minutes.
10. Do a quick release.

11. Gently remove the bowl with the eggs. Cool the eggs and peel them.
12. With a fork, make holes in the egg surface.
13. Add ¼-cup water and coconut milk.
14. Add back the peeled eggs in the pot.
15. Press Sauté and stir fry for 3 minutes.
16. Turn off the IP.
17. Add lemon juice and garnish with cilantro.
18. Serve.

Nutritional Facts Per Serving

- Calories: 268
- Fat: 20g
- Carb: 13g
- Protein: 10g

This is a hearty lamb curry with vegetables.

Lamb Curry (Indian)

Cook time: 20 minutes	Servings: 2

Ingredients

- Cubed lamb stew meat – ½ lb.
- Garlic - 2 cloves, minced
- Fresh ginger – ½ inch, grated
- Coconut milk – 2 tbsps.
- Juice of – ½ lime

- Salt to taste
- Black pepper to taste
- Ghee – ½ tbsp.
- Diced tomatoes – 5 oz.
- Garam masala – 1 ½ tsps.
- Turmeric – 1 pinch
- Onion – 1/3, chopped
- Carrot – 1, chopped
- Zucchini – ½, chopped
- Cilantro to taste, chopped

Method

1. In a bowl, meat, combine lime juice, sea salt, black pepper, milk, ginger, and garlic. Cover and marinate in the refrigerator for 30 minutes or overnight.
2. Add the meat, marinate, ghee, garam masala, tomatoes with their juice, onion, and carrots in the IP.
3. Cover and cook on High for 20 minutes.
4. Do a natural release.
5. Open and press sauté.
6. Stir in diced zucchini and simmer for 5 to 6 minutes.
7. Garnish with chopped cilantro and serve.

Nutritional Facts Per Serving

- Calories: 230
- Fat: 9g
- Carb: 11g
- Protein: 25g

CHAPTER 9 CURRIES

With an Instant Pot, making curry doesn't have to be difficult. This recipe uses simple ingredients and produces a great tasting curry for weeknight emergencies.

Coconut Chicken Curry (Thai)

Cook time: 15	Servings: 2

Ingredients

- Full-fat coconut milk – 1/3 can
- Bone broth – ¼ cup
- Red curry paste – 1 ½ tsps.
- Fish sauce – ½ tbsp.
- Cracked black pepper – 1/3 tsp.
- Onion – 1/3, chopped
- Red bell peppers – 2/3, sliced
- Carrot – 1, chopped
- Green beans – ½ cup, chopped
- Garlic – 1 clove, chopped
- Fresh ginger – 1/3 inch, minced
- Chicken thighs – ½ lb.
- Juice of ½ lime
- Chopped basil to taste

Method

1. Place fish sauce, curry paste, bone broth, milk, and black pepper in the Instant Pot and whisk to mix.
2. Add chicken, ginger, garlic, green beans, carrots, bell peppers, and onion. Stir to mix.
3. Cover and press Poultry. Cook for 10 minutes.
4. Release pressure naturally when cooked.
5. Remove the chicken and shred it.
6. Add it back in the pot and mix.
7. Top with basil and lime juice.
8. Serve with rice.

Nutritional Facts Per Serving

- Calories: 464
- Fat: 35g
- Carb: 14g
- Protein: 22g

This is a Vietnamese sweet and salty braised pork recipe. You can use pork shoulder for a leaner version and coconut water if you can't find coconut soda.

Vietnamese Caramelized Pork

Cook time: 45 to 50 minutes	Servings: 2

Ingredients

- Pork belly – 2/3 lb. cut into 2-inch pieces
- Hard-boiled eggs – 2
- Sugar – 1/8 cup
- Garlic – 1 clove, chopped
- Shallot – 1/3, chopped
- Star anise pods – 1
- Black pepper – 1/3 tsp.
- Salt – 2/3 tsp.

- Soy sauce – ¼ tbsp.
- Coconut (flavored soda) – 4 ounces
- Water – 1 cup
- Fish sauce – 1/3 tsp.

Method

1. In a bowl, combine the soy sauce, black pepper, salt, shallot, garlic, and pork. Set aside to marinate.
2. Press sauté on high.
3. Add the marinated pork and sauté for 5 to 7 minutes, or until pork gets some color.
4. Deglaze with water and turn off the pot.
5. To make the sauce: caramelize the sugar in a pan until dark brown. Add ¼ cup water and mix to make a sauce.
6. Add the star anise pod, coconut soda, hard-boiled eggs and enough water to cover the pork.
7. Cook for 30 minutes on high pressure. Then do a natural release.
8. Add the fish salt and adjust seasoning.
9. Serve over rice.

Nutritional Facts Per Serving

- Calories: 524
- Fat: 28g
- Carb: 31.4g
- Protein: 40.6g

This flavorful and delicious Vietnamese chicken curry dish is a favorite choice for most Vietnamese people. The use of coconut milk is the defining characteristic of this curry dish.

Vietnamese Chicken Curry (Ca Ri Ga)

Cook time: 16 minutes	Servings: 2

Ingredients

- Chicken thighs – ¾ pound, boneless and skinless, cut into 3 to 4-inch pieces
- Lemongrass stalks – 1, cut into pieces and pounded
- Coconut milk – 7 ounces

- Carrots – 2, chopped
- Potatoes – 2, peeled and chopped
- Onion – ½ diced
- Garlic – 2 cloves, minced
- Yellow curry powder – 1 ½ tbsps.
- Fish sauce – 1 ½ tbsps.
- Freshly grated ginger – ½ tsp.
- Granulated sugar – 1 tsp.
- Salt – ½ tsp.
- Bay leaf – 1
- Coconut oil – ½ tbsp.
- All-purpose flour – 1 tbsp.
- Cilantro for garnish

Method

1. In a bowl, add the ginger, garlic, salt, ½ of the curry powder, and chicken and marinate for at least 1 hour.
2. Press sauté on the Instant Pot and add coconut oil.
3. Brown the chicken on all sides for 5 minutes.
4. Set aside the chicken to one side.
5. Add the onions and cook until soft, about 3 minutes.
6. Add the flour and coat the chicken well.
7. Add the coconut milk, remaining curry powder, fish sauce, sugar, bay leaf, and lemongrass.
8. Cover and cook on Manual for 2 minutes on High pressure.
9. Once cooked, do a natural release and open the pot.
10. Add the carrots and potatoes and mix.
11. Cover and cook on Manual for 4 minutes on High pressure.
12. Do a natural release.

13. Check the seasoning and serve over Jasmine rice or French bread.
14. Garnish with cilantro and enjoy.

Nutritional Facts Per Serving

- Calories: 608
- Fat: 31.7g
- Carb: 45.7g
- Protein: 39.2g

This butter chicken is easy to make and flavorful. The recipe tastes just like a restaurant meal and a family favorite. This dish has the perfect blend of masala, creaminess and tomato flavor.

Indian Butter Chicken

Cook time: 25 minutes	Servings: 2

Ingredients

- Ghee – 1 tbsp.
- Onion – ½ diced
- Minced garlic – 2 tsps.
- Minced ginger – ½ tsp.
- Skinless and boneless chicken thighs – ¾ pound, cut into quarters

Spices

- Coriander powder – ½ tsp.
- Garam masala – ½ tsp.
- Paprika – ½ tsp.
- Salt – ½ tsp.
- Turmeric – ½ tsp.
- Black pepper – 1 pinch
- Cayenne – 1 pinch
- Ground cumin – 1 pinch
- Tomato sauce – 6 ounces

Add later

- Chopped green bell peppers
- Heavy cream
- Fenugreek leaves
- Cilantro

(All are to taste)

Method

1. Press the sauté and add the ghee and onion to the Instant Pot.
2. Stir-fry onions until beginning to brown, about 6 to 7 minutes.
3. Add ginger, garlic, and chicken. Stir-fry the chicken until the outside is no longer pink, about 6 to 7 minutes.
4. Add the spices and mix.
5. Stir in the tomato sauce and cover with the lid.
6. Cook on high pressure for 10 minutes.
7. Do a quick release and open the lid.
8. Press sauté and the bell peppers and cook until soft.
9. Stir in the fenugreek leaves and cream.

10. Garnish with cilantro and serve.

Nutritional Facts Per Serving

- Calories: 243
- Fat: 15.7g
- Carb: 14.4g
- Protein: 12.1g

Kari Ayam – This is an Indonesian chicken curry recipe. Usually, it takes an hour to cook on stove top, but with Instant Pot, it takes only minutes.

Indonesian Curry Chicken (Kari Ayam)

Cook time: 15 minutes	Servings: 2

Ingredients

- Bone-in, skin-on drumettes, and wings (separated) – 1 lb. discard the tip
- Cooking oil – ½ tbsp.
- Onion – 1/3, chopped
- Garlic – 1 clove, chopped

- Kaffir Lime leaves – 1, edges tore to release flavor
- Curry leaves – a few
- Turmeric powder – 1/3 tsp.
- Small star anise – 1
- All-purpose chili sauce – 1/3 tbsp.
- Water – ½ cup
- Roma tomatoes – 1 halved
- Coconut cream – 1/3 cup
- Salt to taste

Method

1. Press sauté and add oil. Add garlic and onion to the hot oil and stir-fry for 1 minute. Add turmeric, curry leaves, lime leaves, and star anise. Stir-fry for another minute. Add the chicken pieces and mix well.
2. Pour in the water and add tomatoes.
3. Close the lid and cook on High pressure for 15 minutes.
4. When cooked, do a quick release.
5. Remove the lid, stir in the coconut cream and mix well.
6. Season with salt.
7. Serve.

Nutritional Facts Per Serving

- Calories: 242
- Fat: 9.5g
- Carb: 4.7g
- Protein: 32.7g

This is a super easy classic beef curry. Cooking in IP makes a creamy hearty tender beef curry.

Beef Curry (Hong Kong)

Cook time: 35 minutes	Servings: 2

Ingredients

- Beef finger meat – 1 pound
- Potato – ½, chopped
- Unsalted chicken stock – ½ cup

- Coconut milk – 2 tbsps.
- Chu Hou Sauce – 1 tbsp.
- Curry powder – 1 tbsp.
- Bay leaves – 1
- Garlic cloves – 2
- Shallot – ½
- Fish sauce – ½ tbsp.
- White sugar – ½ tsp.

Thickener

- Cornstarch – 1 tbsp.
- Cold water – 2 tbsp.

Method

1. Press sauté on your IP and add oil.
2. Brown the meat in the IP. About 2 minutes on each side. Set aside.
3. Add shallot, garlic, and bay leaves in the IP. Stir-fry for a few minutes.
4. Cut the beef in bit size pieces.
5. Add the chu hou sauce, fish sauce, sugar, curry powder, and meat pieces in the IP. Stir fry for 1 minute. Add a bit of chicken stock and deglaze the pot.
6. Add the potato and mix well.
7. Cover and cook on High for 25 minutes, then do a natural release for 15 minutes.
8. Remove the beef and half of the potato chunks.
9. Press sauté and add coconut milk.
10. Mix and add the cornstarch with water.
11. Mix and adjust seasoning.
12. Add back the beef and potato to the pot.
13. Mix and serve.

Nutritional Facts Per Serving

- Calories: 336
- Fat: 15g
- Carb: 18.4g
- Protein: 32.1g

This spicy, flavorful, authentic Sri Lankan curry recipe can be made with or without coconut milk.

Chicken Curry

Cook time: 15 minutes	Servings: 2

Ingredients

- Coconut oil – 1 tbsp.
- Onion – 2 tbsps.
- Garlic – 1 clove, minced

- Ginger – 1/3 inch, minced
- Bay leave – 1
- Roasted Sri Lankan curry powder – ½ tbsp.
- Cinnamon – ½ stick
- Salt – a pinch
- Cayenne pepper – 1/3 tsp.
- Paprika – 1/3 tbsp.
- Chicken – 2/3 lb. thigh or leg pieces
- Serrano pepper – ½
- Roma tomatoes – 1 sliced
- Brown sugar – ½ tbsp.
- Apple cider vinegar – ½ tsp.
- Coconut milk – 2 tbsps.
- Water – 2 tbsps.

Method

1. In the Instant Pot add the coconut oil and heat.
2. Add ginger, garlic, and onion to the heated oil and cook until softened.
3. Add chili or cayenne pepper, curry powder, curry leaves, cinnamon, and paprika. Cook for a few minutes.
4. Add the sugar, tomato, salt, green chili/serrano peppers, and chicken. Mix to coat.
5. Cover and cook on High pressure for 10 minutes.
6. Do a natural release.

Nutritional Facts Per Serving

- Calories: 265
- Fat: 12.9g
- Carb: 3.3g

- Protein: 32.3g

This is a quick and easy Sri Lankan style chicken curry recipe.

Chicken Curry

Cook time: 15 minutes	Servings: 2

Ingredients

- Onion – 1, chopped
- Tomato – 1 chopped
- Garlic – 1 chopped
- Ginger – ½ inch chopped
- Curry leaf – 1
- Pandan leaf – 1
- Lemongrass – 1
- Cardamom – 3
- Cinnamon – ½ piece
- Chicken – 1 lb. cut up

- Canola oil – 1 tsp.
- Curry powder – ½ tbsp.
- Red chili powder – ½ tbsp.
- Salt – 1 tsp.
- Green mango powder – ½ tbsp.

Method

1. Add the oil in the Instant Pot and rest of the ingredients. Mix and do not add water.
2. Cover and cook on High pressure for 15 minutes.
3. Do a quick pressure release.
4. Enjoy.

Nutritional Facts Per Serving

- Calories: 319
- Fat: 8.4g
- Carb: 15.8g
- Protein:44.7g

This Instant Pot Burmese beef potato curry is simple. Using aromatic spices and herbs makes it delicious.

Beef Potato Curry

Cook time: 50 minutes	Servings: 2

Ingredients

- Beef stew meat – 350 grams
- Potatoes – 150 grams, chopped
- Cooking oil – 1 tbsp.
- Onion – 1/3, diced

- Grated ginger – ½ tbsp.
- Garlic – 1 clove, minced
- Large tomato – 1/3 diced
- Water – 1/3 cup

Spices

- Turmeric – ½ tbsp.
- Madras curry powder – 1/3 tbsp.
- Cumin powder – 1/3 tsp.
- Cinnamon – 1/3 stick
- Paprika – ½ tbsp.

Herbs

- Bay leaves – 1
- Fresh cilantro leaves

Seasoning

- Salt – ½ tsp.
- Sugar – 1/3 tsp.

Serve with

- Lemons – 1, cut into wedges

Method

1. Press sauté on the IP.
2. Add oil and garlic, ginger, and onion.
3. Stir-fry for 3 minutes.
4. Add spices and tomato pieces and stir-fry for 2 minutes more.
5. Add the bay leaf, beef, and seasoning. Mix.
6. Add ½-cup water.
7. Cover and cook on High for 30 minutes.

8. Do a quick release and open.
9. Pres sauté. Add potato pieces and mix.
10. Cook for 15 to 20 minutes or until the potatoes are soft.
11. Taste and adjust seasoning.
12. Serve.

Nutritional Facts Per Serving

- Calories: 263
- Fat: 12.6g
- Carb: 17g
- Protein: 20.2g

This Mongolian beef recipe gets better when cooked in a traditional Chinese away.

Mongolian Beef

Cook time: 20 minutes	Servings: 2

Ingredients

- Coconut oil – ½ tbsp.
- Long red chili – 2 slices
- Grated ginger - 1 tsp.
- Beef skirt steak or flank steak – 250 grams, cut into thin strips
- Garlic – 2 cloves, grated
- Tamari sauce – 2 tbspss.
- Coconut sugar – 2 tbsps.
- Honey – ½ tbsp.

- Sesame oil – ½ tsp.
- Fish sauce – ½ tsp.

To finish it off

- Tapioca flour – 1 tbsp.
- Carrot – 1, cut into matchsticks
- Green onions – 1, cut into long pieces (green and pale green part only)
- Cooked rice to serve

Method

1. Press Sauté on your IP.
2. Add oil, then add chili and ginger and stir to mix.
3. Add garlic and beef strips. Cook and stir for 1 minute.
4. Except for the green onion, carrots, and tapioca, add the rest of the ingredients.
5. Cancel Sauté.
6. Cover and cook on Manual for 12 minutes on High.
7. Do a natural pressure release and open the lid.
8. Add the carrots and press Sauté.
9. Cook for 2 minutes.
10. In the meantime, combine tapioca with ¼-cup hot water in a bowl. Mix.
11. Add 4 tbsps. of a tapioca-water mixture and green onions the IP.
12. Mix and press cancel.
13. Serve with cauliflower rice or cooked rice.

Nutritional Facts Per Serving

- Calories: 228
- Fat: 9.3g

- Carb: 20.9g
- Protein: 17.6g

CHAPTER 10 SALAD RECIPES

This delicious recipe is made unique with the use of Vietnamese coriander. This salad dish is perfect for a cold or a rainy day.

Vietnamese Chicken Porridge & Salad (Cháo & Gỏi Gà)

Cook time: 25 to 30 minutes	Servings: 2

Ingredients for chicken porridge

- Chicken leg quarters – 2 (prepared)

- Jasmine rice - ½ cup (washed well)
- Ginger – 1 inch, sliced
- Onion – ½, quartered
- Shallot – 1, quartered
- Chicken soup base – 2 tbsp.
- Boiling water – 2 to 4 cups (depends how thick you want)
- Sugar, salt, mushroom seasoning, fish sauce to taste

Chicken salad

- Onion – ½, sliced
- Cabbage – ¼, finely shredded
- Vietnamese coriander – a few, chopped
- Fried shallot

Salad dressing

- Ginger – ½ inch, sliced
- Minced garlic – ½ tbsp.
- Fish sauce – 1 tbsp.
- Sugar – 1 tbsp.
- Lime juice - 1 tbsp.

Garnishes

- Fried shallot, chili, black pepper, chopped onion, and cilantro

Method

1. Season the chicken with salt.
2. In the Instant Pot, add soup base, ginger, shallot, onion, and chicken.
3. Pour boiling water to cover the ingredients.
4. Cover and press Manual. Cook on high pressure for 8 minutes, then do a natural release for 5 minutes.

5. Meanwhile, mix lime juice, sugar, and sauce to make the salad dressing. Add garlic and ginger and mix. Adjust seasoning and set aside.
6. Remove chicken and put it in cold water to stop cooking. Drain and set aside.
7. Remove shallot and onion from the broth and add soup base and rice.
8. Mix and cover.
9. Press Porridge and cook for 18 minutes. Do a natural release when cooked.
10. Meanwhile, shred chicken and mix with coriander, sliced onion, and cabbage.
11. Drizzle with dressing and toss to combine.
12. Open the lid and stir the porridge. Adjust seasoning if necessary.
13. On serving plates, arrange the porridge, and chicken.
14. Garnish and serve.

Nutritional Facts Per Serving

- Calories: 408
- Fat: 3.2g
- Carb: 66.7g
- Protein: 28.5g

Japanese Potato Salad

Cook time: 4 minutes	Servings: 2

Ingredients

- Russet potato – 1 medium, diced
- Kewpie Mayonnaise – 2 tbsps.
- Diced onions – 1 tbsp.
- Carrot – 1 tbsp. chopped
- Japanese cucumber – 1/3 thinly sliced
- Salt – ½ tsp. Divided
- Granulated sugar – a pinch
- Rice vinegar – ½ tsp.

Method

1. Sprinkle the cucumber slices with salt. Coat well and set aside for 10 minutes. Then squeeze out as much as liquid possible with paper towels.
2. Place 1 cup water into the IP.
3. Place the steamer basket in the IP.
4. Place the diced potatoes into the steamer basket.
5. Close and cook on Manual for 4 minutes on High.
6. Do a quick release. Open the lid and remove the potatoes.
7. Cool and drain the potatoes for a few minutes.
8. In a bowl, add rice vinegar, sugar, salt, and mayonnaise. Mix well.
9. Add the cucumber, carrots, onions, and potatoes.
10. Mix with a spoon.
11. Taste and adjust seasoning.
12. Refrigerate uncovered for 2 hours before serving.

Nutritional Facts Per Serving

- Calories: 134
- Fat: 5.1g
- Carb: 21g
- Protein: 2.3g

This salad recipe is easy to make. You cook the pork loin in IP. Then toss with cooked quinoa, cashews, green onions, cilantro, and cabbage.

Chopped Chinese Pork Salad

Cook time: 50 minutes	Servings: 2

Ingredients

- Pork loin – ½ lb. quartered
- Water – ¼ cup
- Soy sauce - 1 tbsp.
- Sesame oil – 1 tsp.
- Garlic powder – ¼ tsp.
- Fresh ginger – ½ tsp. grated
- Chinese 5 spice powder - a pinch
- Brown sugar – ½ tsp.

For the salad

- Cooked quinoa – ½ cup
- Shredded or chopped cabbage – ¼ lb.
- Carrot – ½, chopped
- Green onions – ½, chopped
- Cashews – 1 tbsp.
- Tamari sunflower seeds – ½ tsp.
- Chopped cilantro – 1 tbsp.

For the dressing

- Fresh lime juice to taste
- Soy sauce to taste
- Rice vinegar to taste
- Sesame seeds to taste
- Sesame oil to taste
- Sugar to taste
- Salt – to taste
- Vegetable oil to taste

Method

1. Make the pork: Place the chopped pork in the IP.
2. In a bowl, combine brown sugar, water, 5 spice, ginger, garlic powder, sesame oil, and tamari. Mix to make it smooth and pour over the meat.
3. Cover and cook on High for 50 minutes.
4. Prepare salad ingredients: While the pork is cooking, chop up every salad ingredients and place in a bowl.
5. Whisk all the salad dressing ingredients in a bowl and set aside.
6. When cooking is done, do a natural release.
7. Prepare the salad and serve.

Nutritional Facts Per Serving

- Calories: 428
- Fat: 15.4g
- Carb: 34.2g
- Protein: 37.7g

This crunchy Paleo and Whole30 Chinese chicken salad is packed with vegetables and full of texture.

Paleo Chinese Chicken Salad

Cook time: 20 minutes	Servings: 2

Ingredients for the chicken

- Chicken thighs – ½ lb.
- Salt and pepper to taste
- Bone broth – ¼ cup

For the dressing

- Juice of ½ orange
- Olive oil – ½ tbsp.
- Coconut aminos – ½ tbsp.
- Dijon mustard – ½ tbsp.
- Rice wine vinegar – ¼ tbsp.
- Sesame oil – ¼ tsp.

For the salad

- Cabbage – ¼ cup, chopped
- Kale – 1 cup
- Celery – ¼ cup
- Carrots – ½, chopped
- Green onions – 1 ½ tbsps. diced
- Slivered almonds – 1 tbsp.

Method

1. Season the chicken with salt and pepper.
2. Place the chicken in the IP.
3. Add bone broth and cook for 20 minutes on High.
4. Remove the chicken and shred with two forks.
5. Combine all the dressing ingredients in a bowl.
6. Prep the rest of the ingredients.
7. Place all of the vegetables and chicken in a large bowl.
8. Toss to mix.
9. Add the dressing, top with slivered almonds and serve.

Nutritional Facts Per Serving

- Calories: 315
- Fat: 15.4g

- Carb: 6.6g
- Protein: 36.1g

Enjoy this summer heat with this Asian noodle salad. You could make this with any type of pasta.

Asian Sesame Noodle Salad

Cook time: 10 minutes	Servings: 2

Ingredients for the noodle

- Linguine – 1/3 lb.
- Water – 1 ½ cups

Peanut dressing

- Smooth peanut butter – 1 tbsp.
- Tamari – 1 tbsp.
- Warm water – 2 tbsps.
- Peeled fresh ginger – ½ tbsp. chopped

- Fresh minced garlic – ½ tsp.
- Rice wine vinegar – ½ tsp.
- Sesame oil – ½ tsp.
- Honey – ½ tsp.
- Crushed chili pepper flakes - 1 pinch

Noodle salad

- Vegetable oil – ½ tbsp.
- Sliced red pepper – 1 tbsp.
- Chopped green onions – 1 tbsp.
- Sesame seeds – ½ tsp. toasted
- Toasted peanuts – 1 tbsp. chopped
- Lime for garnish

Method

1. Press Manual on your IP.
2. Add pasta and water in the IP.
3. Cover and press Manual. Cook on High for 4 minutes.
4. Do a quick release.
5. Open and transfer paste in a bowl.
6. Rinse under cold water.
7. Place in a large bowl.
8. Toss with vegetable oil, then add the green onions and red bell pepper.
9. Puree all the dressing ingredients in a blender.
10. Pour the dressing over the pasta and vegetables.
11. Top with toasted sesame seeds.
12. Top with toasted peanuts and quartered lime and serve.

Nutritional Facts Per Serving

- Calories: 422
- Fat: 21.7g
- Carb: 45.4g
- Protein: 12.8g

This Thai brown rice salad is hearty and nutritious. The vegetables and peanut butter dressing make it delicious.

Thai Brown Rice Salad

Cook time: 15 minutes	Servings: 2

Ingredients

- Uncooked brown rice – ½ cup
- Fresh ginger – 1 slice
- Garlic clove – 1 clove
- Vegetable stock – ½ cube
- Water – ¾ cup

For the salad

- Cabbage – ¼ cup, chopped
- Carrot – 1/2, chopped

- Red bell pepper – 1/2, chopped
- Red onion – ¼, chopped
- Cherry tomatoes – 2, halved
- Black or white sesame seeds – ½ tsp.
- Finish with cilantro/coriander and chopped fresh mint

For the dressing

- Crunchy peanut butter – ½ tbsp.
- Honey – ½ tbsp.
- Minced garlic – 1 clove
- Grated ginger – ½ tsp.
- Red chili – to taste
- Juice of half a lime
- Soy sauce – 1 tbsp.
- Fish sauce – ½ tbsp.
- Sesame oil – ½ tsp.
- Olive oil – ½ tbsp.
- Water – 1 tbsp.
- Lime to serve

Method

1. Add the rice ingredients in the IP and mix.
2. Cover with the lid and press Manual.
3. Cook on High for 15 minutes.
4. Do a natural release for 10 minutes.
5. Open the lid and fluff the rice.
6. Transfer the rice to a bowl and cool down.
7. To make the salad dressing, soften the peanut butter, add the remaining salad ingredients, and whisk until smooth.
8. Serve.

Nutritional Facts Per Serving

- Calories: 287
- Fat: 7.5g
- Carb: 49.7g
- Protein: 7.4g

You can make this Asian Chicken salad in the slow cooker also. This recipe is easy to make and full of flavor.

Asian Chicken Salad

Cook time: 5 minutes	Servings: 2

Ingredients

- Sliced mushrooms – ½ cup
- Chopped carrots – ½ cup
- Red bell pepper – ½, chopped

- Boneless, skinless chicken breasts – ½ pound
- Fresh ginger – ½ tbsp. chopped
- Soy sauce – 1 tbsp.
- Rice wine vinegar – 1 tbsp.
- Honey – 1 tbsp.
- Chicken broth – ¼ cup
- Garlic – 1 clove, minced

Method

1. Place chopped vegetables in the bottom of the IP.
2. Top with chicken breasts.
3. Combine remaining ingredients in a bowl and mix well.
4. Pour sauce over chicken.
5. Cover and press poultry and cook for 5 minutes.
6. Do a quick pressure release.
7. Shred chicken and serve.

Nutritional Facts Per Serving

- Calories: 201
- Fat: 1.8g
- Carb: 16.9g
- Protein: 28.4g

This is delicious Thai quinoa, mango salad. This refreshing summer salad is packed with flavor and makes a great lunch.

Thai Quinoa Mango Salad with Dressing

Cook time: 15 minutes	Servings: 2

Ingredients

- Quinoa – ¼ cup, uncooked
- Red pepper – ¼, chopped
- Medium carrot – ½, chopped
- Green onion – ½ stalk, chopped

- Mango – ½, sliced
- Jalapeno – ¼, chopped
- Cilantro – to taste

Dressing

- Peanut butter – 1 ¼ tbsp.
- Soy sauce – 1/3 tbsp.
- Rice vinegar – ¼ tbsp.
- Lime juice from 1 lime
- Ginger – ¼ tbsp., minced
- Honey – ¾ tbsp.
- Sesame oil – ¼ tsp.
- Sriracha to taste

Method

1. Add quinoa and water in the Instant Pot.
2. Cook for 1 minute on High, then do a natural release.
3. Chop everything and arrange in a bowl.
4. In a bowl, add all the dressing ingredients and mix.
5. Whisk to mix.
6. Pour the dressing over the prepared mango, veggies, and quinoa.
7. Toss the salad with the dressing.
8. Garnish with peanuts and serve.

Nutritional Facts Per Serving

- Calories: 175
- Fat: 6g
- Carb: 23g
- Protein: 6g

This sweet and savory Asian salad recipe is easy to cook in your Instant Pot.

Asian Spaghetti Salad with Dressing

Cook time: 1 minute	Servings: 2

Ingredients for the spaghetti

- Spaghetti noodles – 3 ounces, uncooked
- Water – 1 cup
- Salt to taste

Other ingredients

- Thinly sliced cabbage – 1/3 cup
- Green onion – ¾, chopped
- Avocado – ½ sliced
- Shredded carrots – 1 tbsp.
- Shredded edamame – 2 tbsps.
- Sliced almonds – ½ tbsp.
- Sesame seeds for topping
- Sesame ginger dressing
- Oil – 1 tbsp.
- Rice vinegar – 1 tbsp.
- Soy sauce – 1 tbsp.
- Brown sugar to taste
- Mince garlic – ½ tsp.
- Ground ginger to taste
- Sesame oil to taste

Method

1. To cook the pasta, put noodles, water, and salt in the IP.
1. Close and press Manual.
2. Cook 1 minute.
3. Do a natural release.
4. Open the noodles and drain if necessary. Set aside.
5. Combine almonds, edamame, carrots, avocado, onion, cabbage, and spaghetti.
6. Whisk the dressing ingredients in a bowl and drizzle over the salad.
7. Toss to coat.
8. Sprinkle with sesame seeds and serve.

Nutritional Facts Per Serving

- Calories: 178
- Fat: 12.9g
- Carb: 12.5g
- Protein: 4g

This Asian salad is made with cashews, cilantro, onion, carrots, quinoa, and cabbage and dressed in a vinaigrette dressing.

Asian Slaw Quinoa Salad

Cook time: 12 minutes	Servings: 2

Ingredients

For quinoa

- Quinoa – ½ cup, rinsed
- Water – ½ cup

Other ingredients

- Cabbage – 1 cup, shredded
- Carrots – 2 tbsps. shredded
- Fresh cilantro to taste, chopped
- Cashews – 1 tbsp. toasted and chopped
- Black sesame seeds to taste
- Green onion – ½, sliced, stalk and steam separated

For the vinaigrette

- Rice vinegar – 1 tbsp.
- Fresh ginger to taste, grated
- Garlic to taste, minced
- Maple syrup to taste
- Salt and pepper to taste
- Extra virgin olive oil – 1 tbsp.
- Sesame oil – 1 tsp.

Method

1. Combine the quinoa and water in the Instant Pot and cover.
2. Cook on High pressure for 1 minute.
3. Do a natural release.
4. Open the lid and remove the quinoa in a bowl.
5. In a bowl, combine green onions, seeds, cashews, cilantro, carrots, quinoa, and cabbage.
6. In another bowl, mix the dressing ingredients. Whisk until creamy.
7. Drizzle the salad with dressing and serve.

Nutritional Facts Per Serving

- Calories: 258
- Fat:11.6g
- Carb: 31.4g
- Protein: 7.2g

CHAPTER 11 SAUCES

Once you taste this homemade hoisin sauce, you will never use a store-bought sauce again. Additionally, this sauce is made with commonly available ingredients.

Homemade Hoisin Sauce (Chinese)

Total time: 5 minutes	Yield: ½ cup

Ingredients

- Light soy sauce – ¼ cup
- Natural peanut butter – 2 tbsps.
- Honey – 1 tbsp.
- Rice vinegar – 2 tsps.
- Sesame oil – 2 tsps.
- Garlic – 1 clove, grated
- Black pepper – 1/8 tsp.
- Miso paste – 1 tsp. or five spice powder – ¼ tsp. or Thai chili sauce – 1 tsp.

Method

1. Combine all ingredients in a bowl and mix well.
2. Store in an airtight bottle in the fridge.

Nutritional Facts Per Serving (1 tbsp.)

- Calories: 50
- Fat: 3.2g
- Carb: 3.8g
- Protein: 1.9g

This orange sauce is versatile. You can use it with stir fry, chicken or even roasted vegetables.

Orange Chicken Sauce (Chinese)

Cook time: 5 minutes	Yield:2 ½ cup

Ingredients

- Vegetable oil – 1 tbsp.
- Garlic – 4 cloves, minced
- Minced garlic – 2 tbsps.

Sauce mix

- Dried tangerine peel or grated orange zest – ½ cup (soaked in hot water for 20 minutes, then drained and sliced)
- Orange juice – 1 cup
- Rice vinegar or distilled white vinegar– ¾ cup
- Light soy sauce – ¼ cup
- Shaoxing wine – ¼ cup
- Sugar – ½ cup
- Cornstarch – 2 tbsps. and ½ tbsp.
- Fine sea salt – 1 tsp.

Method

1. In a bowl, add ¼ cup sliced tangerine skin.
2. Add the soaked tangerine skin and the rest of the sauce ingredients to a bowl. Add cornstarch and mix well.
3. Heat oil in a saucepan and add ginger and garlic. Cook until you get a strong fragrance.
4. Stir the sauce again and pour into the pan.
5. Cook and stir until thick.
6. Transfer the sauce into a bowl.
7. Store in an airtight jar when cooled.

Nutritional Facts Per Serving (2 tbsp.)

- Calories: 83
- Fat: 1.1g
- Carb: 17.6g
- Protein: 0.8g

This homemade black bean sauce is extremely popular because it is versatile. You can use it for steaming, grilling, baking, and frying.

Black Bean Sauce (Chinese)

Cook time: 15 minutes	Yields: 2 servings

Ingredients

- Fermented black beans – 1 cup (rinsed, drained, and chopped)
- Vegetable oil – 1/3 cup
- White onion – ¼ cup, minced
- Shaoxing wine – ¼ cup

- Light soy sauce – ¼ cup
- Sugar – ¼ cup
- Garlic – 1 head, minced
- Ginger – 1 thumb, minced

Method

1. In a saucepan, heat oil and dried chili peppers over medium heat until warm.
2. Lower heat and cook and stir until chili peppers are dark, but not black.
3. Discard the chili peppers.
4. Add the onion and black beans.
5. Cook and stir until the sauce appears dry.
6. Add sugar, soy sauce, and wine. Simmer and stir for about 10 minutes or until onion is tender. Careful not to burn the sauce.
7. Add ginger and garlic, cook and stir until the onion is very tender.
8. Transfer the sauce to a bowl and cool completely.
9. Store the sauce in an airtight jar in the fridge.

Nutritional Facts for Entire Recipe

- Calories: 1612
- Fat: 75.8g
- Carb: 185.5g
- Protein: 47.1g

This is a traditional white sauce and popular in the Philippines.

Filipino White Sauce Recipe

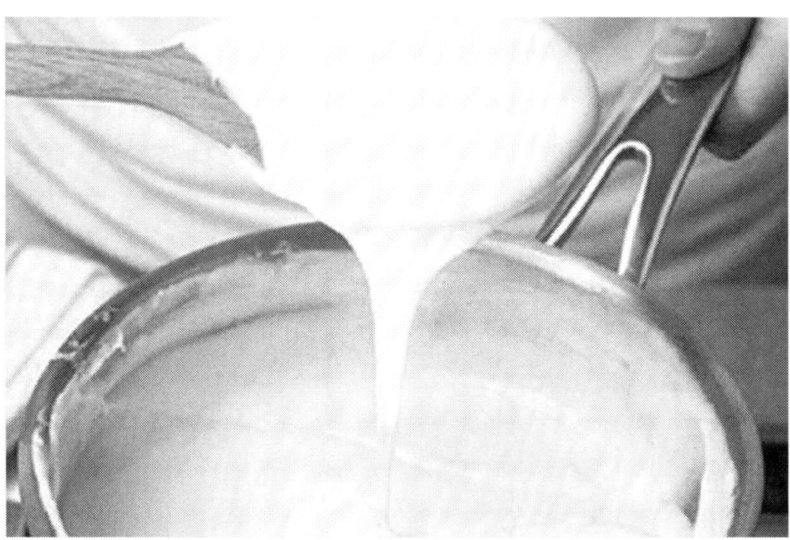

Cook time: 10 minutes	Yields: 2 cups

Ingredients

- Flour – ¼ cup
- Butter – ¼ cup
- Milk – 2 cups
- Salt – ½ tsp.

Method

1. Add the butter in a saucepan and melt over low heat.
2. Add flour and mix.

3. Slowly add milk and stir.
4. Add salt and cook until thickens.

Nutritional Facts for The Entire Recipe

- Calories: 765
- Fat: 56.3g
- Carb: 47.9g
- Protein: 19.7g

This great tasting Japanese sweet and sour stir-fry sauce will be your go-to stir-fry sauce.

Japanese Sweet and Sour Sauce

Ready in: 11 minutes	Yield: 1 cup

Ingredients

- Vinegar – 4 tbsps.
- Soy sauce – 4 tbsps.
- Brown sugar – 6 tbsps.
- Salt – 2 tsp.
- Water – 2/3 cup
- Garlic powder – 1 dash
- Ginger - dash
- Cornstarch to thicken

Method

1. In a saucepan, mix ginger, garlic, water, salt, sugar, soy sauce, and vinegar.
2. Heat on the stove.
3. Add cornstarch to thicken and use as a dipping sauce.
4. Or you can avoid including cornstarch and use it as a stir-fry sauce.

Nutritional Facts Per Serving (387 gram)

- Calories: 371.4
- Fat: 0.1g
- Carb: 85.9g
- Protein: 7.8g

This gochujang sauce is a popular sauce in Korea. It is used in Korean bulgogi, sandwiches, tacos, rice bowls and more.

Spicy Korean Bibimbap Sauce

Cook time: 0 minutes	Yield: ¾ cup

Ingredients

- Korean red-hot pepper paste – 4 tbsps.
- Sesame oil – 2 tbsps.
- Brown sugar – 2 tbsps.
- Soy sauce – 1 tbsp.
- Water – 1 tbsp.
- Rice vinegar – 2 tsps.
- Minced garlic – 2 tsps.

- Toasted sesame seeds – 1 tbsp.

Method

1. In a bowl, add the ingredients and whisk to combine.
2. Cover and keep in the refrigerator.

Nutritional Facts for the Entire Recipe

- Calories: 536
- Fat: 32.9g
- Carb: 58.8g
- Protein: 7.8g

Cincalok is a Malaysian dipping sauce. The sauce is made using fermented tiny shrimp. Beginners may not like the odor of the sauce, but once mixed it is actually great when added to lime juice and other ingredients.

Cincalok Dipping Sauce

Total time: 5 minutes	Servings: ½ cup

Ingredients

- Malaysian fermented tiny shrimp - 1/8 cup
- Fresh lime juice – ½ of a lime
- Fresh small red chilies – 1 or 2, prepared
- Garlic – 1 clove, minced
- Shallot – 1 small, finely sliced

Method

1. In a bowl, add the ingredients and mix well.
2. Use with your dishes.

Nutritional Facts for the Entire Recipe

- Calories: 119
- Fat: 1.8g
- Carb: 7.8g
- Protein: 19.9g

There are several versions of chili sauces in Thailand. They are also known as Nam prik pao chili sauce. This sauce is best with noodle dishes, soups and anything you want to spice up.

Thai Chili Sauce (Nam Prik Pao)

Cook time: 8 minutes	Yield: 1 small jar (6 portions)

Ingredients

- Coconut or canola oil – ¼ cup, plus a little more
- Garlic – 4 cloves, chopped
- Shallots -2, chopped
- Dried whole or crushed red chilies – 3 tbsps. powdered
- Shrimp paste – 1 tsp.
- Fish sauce – 2 tbsps.
- Palm or brown sugar – 2 to 3 tbsps.
- Tamarind paste – 1 tsp.

- Lime juice 1 ½ tbsps.

Method

1. In a pan, heat oil over a medium heat.
2. Add the garlic and shallots. Fry for 2 to 3 minutes.
3. Remove shallots and garlic and place in a bowl (Keep the oil in the pan).
4. In a food processor, combine prepared chili with the water, lime, tamarind, sugar, fish sauce, and shrimp paste. Add the fried shallots and garlic.
5. Pulse to make a thick paste.
6. Return the paste to the frying pan and mix with the oil over low heat.
7. Gently simmer until you get an even consistency.
8. Add a little water or oil to adjust the consistency.
9. Taste and adjust the sauce.

Nutritional Facts for the Entire Recipe

- Calories: 700
- Fat:55.4g
- Carb: 47.4g
- Protein: 9.2g

This sweet chili sauce is available in Asian food markets. However, instead of buying store brands; make this easy recipe on your own. This sweet Thai chili sauce goes well with many Thai dishes and excellent with fish, seafood, and chicken.

Thai Sweet Chili Sauce (Nam him kai)

Cook time: 15 minutes	Yield: ½ cup

Ingredients

- White or rice vinegar – ½ cup
- White sugar – ½ cup plus 2 tbsps.
- Water – ¼ cup
- Fish sauce – 3 tbsps.
- Sherry – 2 tbsps.
- Garlic – 3 cloves, minced
- Dried crushed chili – ½ to 1 tbsp.
- Cornstarch – 1 ½ tbsps. dissolved in 3 to 4 tbsps. cool water

Method

1. Except for the cornstarch-water mixture, place all ingredients in a saucepan.
2. Bring to a rolling boil.
3. Lower heat to medium and boil until reduced by half, about 10 minutes.
4. Lower heat to low and add the water-cornstarch mixture.
5. Cook and stir for 2 minutes.
6. Remove from heat and taste.
7. Cool and store in a jar.

Nutritional Facts for the Entire Recipe

- Calories: 566
- Fat: 1g
- Carb: 135g
- Protein: 3g

Most Western peanut sauces are made from peanut butter. But this Thai peanut sauce is made with real peanuts. You can use this with beef, chicken or as a dip for vegetables.

Salty Thai Peanut Sauce

Cook time: 0 minute	Servings: 4 to 6 as a dip

Ingredients

- Dry roasted peanuts – 1 cup (unsalted)
- Water – 1/3 cup
- Garlic – 2 cloves, minced
- Dark soy sauce – ½ tsp.
- Sesame oil – 2 tsp.
- Brown sugar – 1 to 2 tbsp.
- Fish sauce – 2 to 12 ½ tbsp.
- Tamarind paste – ½ tsp.
- Cayenne pepper – ½ tsp.

- Coconut milk – 1/3 cup

Method

1. Place all the ingredients in a food processor.
2. Process until smooth.
3. Taste and adjust salt, lime juice, sugar or fish sauce.
4. Serve.

Nutritional Facts Per Serving

- Calories: 237
- Fat: 17g
- Carb: 17g
- Protein: 9g

CHAPTER 12 SOUPS AND STEWS

This is a warming and hearty Korean short rib soup. Traditionally it is slow cooked for hours, but you can also cook it in an Instant Pot.

Short Rib Soup (Galbitang in Korean)

Cook time: 30 minutes	Servings: 2

Ingredients

- Beef short ribs – 0.6 lb. excess fat trimmed
- Water – 3.2 cups
- Yellow onion – 0.4, with skin
- Green onion – 0.8, for cooking broth
- Green onion – 0.8, for garnish, chopped
- Ginger – 0.8 inch, sliced
- Korean radish – 0.2, cut into chunks
- Garlic – 0.8 tbsp. chopped
- Guk ganjang – 0.8 tsp. (Korean soy sauce)
- Korean sea salt – 0.4 tsp.

Method

1. Soak ribs in cold water for an hour to remove excess blood.
2. Meanwhile prep the onions, ginger, and radish.
3. In the Instant Pot, add the yellow onion, ribs, ginger, green onion, radish, and water.
4. Close and press Soup. It will cook for 30 minutes.
5. Once done, release the pressure and open.
6. Skim off fat from soup.
7. Season with salt, garlic, and guk.
8. Serve.

Nutritional Facts Per Serving

- Calories: 990
- Fat: 51g
- Carb: 30g
- Protein: 99g

This is an Indonesian noodle soup recipe, cooked with chicken and vegetables.

Indonesian Chicken Noodle Soup (Mie Sop Ayam Medan)

Cook time: 30 minutes	Servings: 2

Ingredients

- Egg noodles – ½ lb. cooked according to package directions
- Rice noodle stick – ½ lb.
- Cooking oil – ½ tbsp.
- Bone-in, skin-on chicken – 1 ½ lbs. thighs, leg or drumsticks
- Cinnamon – ½ stick

- Lemongrass – 1 stalk, prepared
- Chinese or regular celery – 1 ½ stalks
- Water – 4 cups
- Better than bouillon – ½ tbsp.
- Salt to taste
- Cooking oil for frying

To be ground in a food processor
- Shallots – 5, peeled
- Garlic – ½ blub

Spices and herbs
- Cardamoms – 1 ½
- Bay leaves – 3
- Cloves – 5
- Star anise – ½
- Whole white peppercorns – ½ tsp.

Garnishes
- Chinese celery – 1 bunch, chopped
- Fried shallots crisp
- Indonesian sweet soy sauce to drizzle

Green Chili
- Green chili – 25 grams
- Salt – 1/8 tsp.

Method

1. Destem the green chili and boil in water for 5 minutes or until soft. Add to a blender with salt and blend until a paste.
2. Press sauté on the Instant Pot.

3. Heat 1 tbsp. oil in a skillet and sauté ground spices for 1 minute or until fragrant.
4. Add the chicken, lemongrass, cinnamon, and water to the pot. Add all the herbs and spices.
5. Close and cook on high pressure for 20 minutes.
6. Release pressure naturally when cooked.
7. Remove the chicken and set aside before frying. Strain the soup and discard the solids.
8. Deep-fry the chicken until golden brown. You already cooked the chicken so deep-fry to get the color.
9. Arrange chicken with noodles. Garnish with chopped celery leaves, sweet soy sauce and fried shallot crisps.
10. Serve with chili on the side.

Nutritional Facts Per Serving

- Calories: 741
- Fat: 10.9g
- Carb: 128.5g
- Protein: 49.7g

This is a traditional Korean spicy beef soup. Usually difficult, Instant Pot makes it hassle-free. Made with beef, vegetables, and mild spices, this is a household favorite.

Korean Beef Cabbage Radish Soup (Yukgaejang)

Cook time: 10 minutes	Servings: 2

Ingredients

- Beef stew meat – 2 oz. cut thin

- Radish – ¾ cup, cut into squares
- Small green cabbage – ¼ lb. chopped
- Soybean sprouts (kongnamul) – 1 oz. rinsed and drain
- Green onions – ¼, chopped
- Water – ¾ cup

Seasoning

- Garlic – 2 tsps. Chopped
- Korean soy sauce – ½ tbsp.
- Sea salt – 1/3 tsp.
- Korean red chili pepper – ½ tsp.
- Sesame oil – ½ tsp.
- Garlic powder – ¼ tsp.

Method

1. Press sauté on the Instant Pot and add the sesame oil.
2. Sauté radish for 1 to 2 minutes.
3. Add beef to the IP and also add soy sauce and red chili pepper.
4. Sauté radish and beef until the beef pieces are cooked.
5. Add water, garlic, sprouts, green onions, and cabbage.
6. Add garlic powder, salt and close the lid.
7. Select Soup and cook for the reduced time of 10 minutes.
8. Release pressure naturally.
9. Mix with a ladle and serve with rice.

Nutritional Facts Per Serving

- Calories: 103
- Fat: 5g
- Carb: 7g

- Protein: 7g

Nihari is a one-pot meat stew cooked with a variety of spices. The dish is flavorful, delicious and rich with vitamins and minerals.

Pakistani Beef or Mutton Stew (Nihari)

Cook time: 1 hour 20 minutes	Servings: 2

Ingredients

- Beef or mutton pieces with bone – 200 grams
- Oil – 1 tbsp.
- Garlic paste – ¼ tbsp.
- Ginger paste – ¼ tbsp.
- Salt – ¼ tsp.
- Cumin powder – ¼ tsp.

- Coriander powder – 1 pinch
- Red chili powder – 1 pinch
- Kashmiri chili powder – ¼ tsp.
- Turmeric powder – 1 pinch
- Nihari masala – ½ tbsp.
- Bay leaf – 1
- Grated nutmeg - 1 pinch
- Water – 1 ½ cups
- Black cardamom to taste
- Chilies – ½
- Fried onions – 1 tsp.
- Lemon juice – 1 tsp.
- Flour – 1 tsp. dissolved in 2 tbsps. water

Nihari Masala

- Whole star anise – 1
- Whole long peppers – 1
- Coriander seeds - a few
- Cumin seeds a few
- Fennel seeds a few
- Whole black peppers – 1
- Whole cloves - 1
- Cardamom seeds a few
- Nigella seeds a few
- Cinnamon stick – ½ inch
- Strands mace - ½
- Coriander for garnish
- Ginger slices for garnish

To make the Nihari masala

- Blend all the spices.

Method

1. Heat a pressure cooker and add meat.
2. Add salt, garlic, ginger, and oil.
3. Add the Nihari masala and ground spices.
4. Coat the meat and bones with the spices.
5. Add black cardamom, nutmeg and bay leaf. Mix.
6. Add water.
7. Cover and cook 1 hour on medium heat.
8. Carefully let out air and remove the lid.
9. Add flour-water mixture, lemon juice, fried onions, and chilies.
10. Cook uncovered for 15 minutes.
11. Serve garnish with ginger slices and coriander.

Nutritional Facts Per Serving

- Calories: 206
- Fat: 14g
- Carb: 4g
- Protein: 13g

This is deeply flavorful Chicken Rendang. This Indonesian-Malaysian chicken stew dish is cooked using coconut milk and spices.

Chicken Rendang

Cook time: 45 minutes	Servings: 2

Ingredients

- Boneless, skinless chicken thighs or breasts – 0.75 lbs. cut into cubes
- Cooking oil – 2 tbsp.
- Cinnamon stick – ½
- Cloves – 1 ½, chopped
- Star anise – 1 ½
- Cardamom pods – 1 ½
- Lemongrass – ½, white parts only, pounded and cut into strips
- Coconut milk – ½ cup
- Water – ½ cup
- Kaffir lime leaves – 2 ½ bruised
- Toasted grated coconut kerisik – 2 ½ tbsp.
- Sugar – ½ tbsp.
- Salt to taste

Spice Paste

- Shallots – 3
- Galangal – ½ inch
- Lemongrass – 1 ½ white parts only
- Garlic – 2 cloves
- Ginger – ½ inch
- Dried chilies – 5, seeded

Method

1. Add all the spice paste ingredients in a food processor and blend well.
2. Press sauté and add the oil.

3. Add blended paste to the hot oil and stir-fry for 2 to 3 minutes.
4. Stir in lemongrass, cinnamon, cloves, star anise, cardamom, water, and coconut milk.
5. Add the chicken and mix.
6. Cover and cook on high for 15 minutes.
7. When cooked, do a quick release.
8. Stir in salt, sugar, toasted coconut, and lime leaves.
9. Press sauté and reduce the sauce for 5 minutes. Stirring often.
10. Enjoy.

Nutritional Facts Per Serving

- Calories: 598
- Fat: 38.1g
- Carb: 8.2g
- Protein: 55.5g

This chicken soup is delicious and even better the next day. You can use more spinach with the recipe if you want.

Chicken Gnocchi Soup

Cook time: 20 minutes	Servings: 2

Ingredients

- Chicken breasts – 1
- Chicken stock – 1 cup
- Chopped celery – 1/3 cup
- Chopped onion – ½ cup
- Butter – 1 ½ tbsps.
- Salt and pepper to taste
- Thyme – 1 tsp.

- Half and half – 1 ½ cups
- Shredded carrots – ½ cup
- Gnocchi – ½ package
- Spinach – 1 cup, chopped

Method

1. Press Sauté on your pressure cooker.
2. Sauté the onions and celery in the butter.
3. Add the chicken breasts when the vegetables are ¾ cooked.
4. Then add the thyme and stock.
5. Cover and cook on Manual for 15 minutes on low.
6. Do a quick release and shred the chicken.
7. Press sauté mode and add the carrots and half-and-half.
8. Mix and add the gnocchi.
9. Boil for about 5 minutes or until the gnocchi is cooked through.
10. Add spinach and stir.
11. Serve.

Nutritional Facts Per Serving

- Calories: 461
- Fat: 32.4g
- Carb: 15g
- Protein: 28.2g

This is a simple, but healthy instant pot soup. This beef soup offers a great balance with savory, sour and sweet flavors.

Borscht Soup (Hong Kong)

Cook time: 20 minutes	Servings: 2

Ingredients

- Beef shank – ½ pound
- Cabbage – 200g, cut into pieces
- Onion – ¼, chopped
- Russet potato – ½, chopped
- Tomato – 1, quartered
- Carrot – 1, chopped
- Celery – 1, sliced
- Garlic – 2 cloves

- Bay leaves – 1
- Unsalted chicken stock – 2 cups
- Tomato paste – 1 tbsp.
- Olive oil – ½ tbsp.
- Paprika – 1 tsp.
- Salt and black pepper to taste

Method

1. Press Sauté on your Instant Pot and add oil.
2. Season the beef with salt and pepper and add to the hot oil.
3. Brown the meat on all sides.
4. Remove the meat and add onions to the IP.
5. Sauté for 3 minutes.
6. Then add carrot, garlic, celery, bay leaf, paprika, and tomato sauce.
7. Sauté for 2 minutes then add tomato.
8. Cut the beef into bite size pieces.
9. Add a bit of chicken stock to deglaze the pot.
10. Add back the beef pieces and add the stock.
11. Place potato chunks and cabbage pieces on top.
12. Pressure cook at High for 12 minutes then do a natural release.
13. Open the lid and press sauté.
14. Bring the soup to a boil and gently mix. Boil for 5 minutes more.
15. Taste and adjust seasoning.
16. Serve.

Nutritional Facts Per Serving

- Calories: 237
- Fat: 5g
- Carb: 30g
- Protein: 19g

This is very easy delicious Instant Pot red bean soup from Hong Kong. This soup is comforting and satisfying.

Red Bean Soup (Hong Kong)

Cook time: 50 minutes	Servings: 2

Ingredients

- Adzuki beans – ¼ cup, soaked and drained
- Dried mandarin peel - ½ piece (rehydrated in cold water for 20 minutes) then scrub off the bitter white part
- Cold water – 2 cups
- Brown sugar – 40 grams
- Kosher salt to taste

Method

1. Add the brown sugar, salt, peel, and beans in the pot.
2. Add the water and cook on High pressure for 30 minutes.
3. Do a natural release for 20 minutes.
4. Press sauté and bring the mixture to a boil.
5. Boil until thickens, about 20 minutes. Stir a few times.
6. Taste and adjust seasoning.
7. Serve.

Nutritional Facts Per Serving

- Calories: 142
- Fat: 4g
- Carb: 31g
- Protein: 20g

This classic Korean stew is so flavorful and rich. Known as Kimchi Jjigae, it takes only a fraction of time when cooked in Instant Pot.

Kimchi Jjigae

Cook time: 20 minutes	Servings: 2

Ingredients

- Kimchi – 1 ½ cups, cut up

- Fatty pork or beef – 4 ounces, cut up
- Sesame oil – ½ tbsp.
- Korean red chili pepper flakes – 1 tsp. or to taste
- Juice from kimchi – 2 tbsp.
- Water – 1 cup
- Soy sauce – ½ tbsp.
- Minced garlic – ½ tbsp.
- Tofu- 4 ounces, sliced
- Scallions – 1, chopped
- Black pepper to taste
- Sugar – 1 tsp.

Method

1. Press the sauté on the Instant Pot.
2. Add the kimchi and pork along with the red pepper flakes and sesame oil and cook for 5 minutes.
3. Add the garlic, soy sauce, water, and kimchi juice.
4. Cover and press Soup.
5. Cook for 10 minutes.
6. Open the lid and add scallions and tofu.
7. Cover and cook 5 minutes more.

Nutritional Facts Per Serving

- Calories: 176
- Fat: 7.8g
- Carb: 19.8g
- Protein: 9g

This Indonesian vegetable tamarind soup is called Sayur Asem.

Indonesian Vegetable Tamarind Soup

Cook time: 5 minutes	Servings: 2

Ingredients

- Cooking oil – 1 tsp.
- Raw peanuts – 1 ½ oz.
- Long beans – 1 ½ oz. cut into 2-inch pieces
- Sweet corn – 1, cut into 1-inch pieces
- Large chayotes – 1, cubed
- Cabbage leaves – 3, cut into pieces

- Tomato – 1, quartered
- Bay leaves – 1 or 2
- Water – 4 cups
- Seedless tamarind paste – 1 tbsp. plus 1 ½ tbsp. warm water
- Brown sugar – 1 tbsp.
- Salt to taste

Ground spices

- Galangal – ½ thumb size (mashed and removed after cooking)
- Shallot– 1
- Bird's eye chili – ½
- Red chilies – 2
- Garlic – 1 clove
- Kemiri/candlenuts – 2
- Shrimp paste – ½ tsp.

Method

1. Process all the ground spices in a food processor to make a fine paste. Add a bit of water if needed.
2. Mix warm water and tamarind paste. Get the tamarind juice and discard the solid.
3. Press sauté on your IP. Add oil.
4. Add the paste and stir fry for 1 minute.
5. Add the beef broth and bay leaves.
6. Bring to a boil then add in the rest of the vegetables and other ingredients.
7. Cover and cook on High for 5 minutes.
8. Taste and adjust seasoning.
9. Serve with rice.

Nutritional Facts Per Serving

- Calories: 337
- Fat: 18.8g
- Carb: 37g
- Protein: 10.9g

CHAPTER 13 NOODLES RECIPES

This is a traditional Vietnamese spicy beef noodle soup. The recipe uses a lot of spices, it is comforting and heartwarming.

Spicy Beef Noodle Soup/Bun Bo Hue (Vietnamese)

Cook time: 40 minutes	Servings: 2

Ingredients

Broth ingredients

- Beef shank – 1 lb.
- Oxtail – 2/3 lb.
- Daikon radish – 7 oz.
- Lemongrass – 1 ½ stalk, cut into pieces
- Beef broth powder – 1 tbsp.
- Salt – 1 ½ tsp.
- Fish sauce - 1 ½ tbsps.
- Rock sugar – 2 small

For the spicy soup pasta

- Minced lemongrass – 1 ½ tbsp.
- Vegetable oil – 3 tbsps.
- Minced shallot – ½ tbsp.
- Minced garlic – ½ tbsp.
- Annatto oil – ½ tbsp.
- Hue seasoning powder - ½ tbsp.
- Chili flakes – ¼ tsp.

Noodles and toppings

- Rice noodles – ½ package
- Vietnamese ham – ½ small roll

Method for parboiling

1. Add the oxtail in a pot and fill with water.
2. Bring to a boil. Discard the water and rinse under cold water.

Method

1. In an Instant Pot, place all broth ingredients. Fill the pot with water (up to maximum).
2. Cover and press Stew. Cook for 25 minutes and do a natural release for 15 minutes. Then do a quick release.
3. Remove the beef shank. Place in a bowl with cold water and slice thinly.

To make the spicy soup paste

1. Heat oil in a pan over medium heat.
2. Add lemongrass, shallot, and garlic. Sauté until golden brown.
3. Lower heat and add chili flakes and seasoning. Remove from the heat.
4. Add this paste to the broth.
5. Taste and adjust seasoning.
6. Prepare noodles according to package directions.
7. Arrange and serve

Nutritional Facts Per Serving

- Calories: 386
- Fat: 12.3g
- Carb: 49.5g
- Protein: 20.8g

Indonesian Noodles (Mie Goreng)

Cook time: 15 minutes	Servings: 2

Ingredients

Sauce mixture

- Soy sauce – 1 tbsp.
- Oyster sauce – 1 tbsp.
- Sweet soy sauce – ½ tbsp.
- Sesame oil – ½ tsp.
- Sriracha chili sauce – ½ tsp.
- Low sodium chicken broth – ¼ cup

Mix the above ingredients and set aside

Ingredients

- Egg noodles – 6 oz. prepared according to package instructions. Set aside
- Vegetable oil – 1 tbsp.
- Sesame oil – ½ tsp.
- Shrimps – 6 pieces
- Medium chicken breasts – 1, boneless and skinless, cut into pieces
- Small onion – ½, chopped
- Garlic – 1 clove, chopped
- Grated carrots – ½ cup
- Sliced cabbage or bok choy – 1 cup
- Bean sprouts – ½ cup
- Scallions – 1 stalk, separated green and white parts, sliced
- Salt and pepper to taste

Method

1. Season the shrimp with salt and pepper.
2. Press sauté on the Instant Pot.
3. Add sesame oil and vegetables.
4. Add shrimp and cook 1 minute on each side. Remove the shrimp and set aside.
5. Add the garlic, white parts of scallions, onion, and sliced chicken. Sauté until the chicken is almost cooked. Scrape the bottom of the pot to remove any stuck bits.
6. Add bean sprouts, cabbage, and carrots. Stir –fry for 5 minutes.
7. Add noodles and pour sauce mixture on top.
8. Mix all the ingredients.

9. Cover and cook on High pressure for 5 minutes.
10. Add the shrimps.
11. Serve hot.

Nutritional Facts Per Serving

- Calories: 437
- Fat: 10.6g
- Carb: 54.7g
- Protein: 29.7g

This is Burmese chicken curry soup noodle dish also known as Ono Kyauk-Swé. This is a popular traditional Burmese soup.

Chicken Curry Soup Noodles

Cook time: 20 minutes	Servings: 2

Ingredients

- Corn oil – 1 tbsp.
- Yellow onion – ½, diced
- Garlic – 2 cloves, minced
- Turmeric – 1 tsp.
- Paprika - ½ tsp.
- Chili powder – 1 tsp.
- Chicken stock – 2 cups
- Water – ½ cup

- Fish sauce – 2 tbsps.
- Salt to taste
- Coconut milk – ½ cup
- Egg – 1, beaten
- Hard-boiled egg – 1
- Chickpea flour – 2 tbsps.
- Chicken breast – ½ lb. chopped

Noodles
- Egg noodles for 2, cooked

Garnishes
- Cilantro leaves, hard boiled eggs, red onions, limes, toasted chili flakes, crunchy noodles

Method

1. Press Sauté and add oil.
2. Sauté onions for 4 minutes, then add then the garlic.
3. Stir-fry for 2 minutes, then add the chili flakes, paprika, and turmeric. Stir to combine and make a thick paste.
4. Add the fish sauce and chicken stock and mix.
5. Allow to come up to a slow boil on the Instant Pot.
6. In another bowl, mix water and chickpea flour. Whisk to mix.
7. Mix the beaten egg and coconut milk into this bowl and whisk until creamy.
8. Mix the egg mixture, coconut milk, and the flour mixture into the pot. Add salt.
9. Add the diced chicken meat to the pot and cover.
10. Cook on High pressure for 15 minutes.
11. Do natural release when done and mix in the sliced hard-boiled egg.

12. Cook the egg noodles in another pot according to package instructions.
13. Serve in bowls, garnish with garnish items.

Nutritional Facts Per Serving (without the noodles)

- Calories: 496
- Fat: 35.1g
- Carb: 8g
- Protein: 38.3g

This delicious Chinese garlic Instant Pot noodles recipe is easy to make. This is a quick weeknight meal for you to enjoy.

Garlic Noodles

Cook time: 6 minutes	Servings: 2

Ingredients

- Water – ½ cup
- Chicken broth – ½ cup

- Garlic – 3 cloves, minced
- Soy sauce – 1 tbsp.
- Brown sugar – 1 tbsp.
- Oyster sauce – 1 tbsp.
- Sesame oil – ½ tsp.
- Chili paste – ½ tsp.
- Thin spaghetti noodles – 4 oz. broken in half
- Sesame seeds and green onion for topping

Method

1. In the Instant Pot, combine chili paste, sesame oil, oyster sauce, sugar, soy sauce, garlic, broth, and water. Whisk to mix.
2. Place broken spaghetti noodles on top.
3. Make sure they are covered by the liquid.
4. Cover and cook on High for 6 minutes.
5. Do a quick release.
6. Open the pot and stir noodles.
7. Serve top with green onions and sesame seeds.

Nutritional Facts Per Serving

- Calories: 251
- Fat: 3.1g
- Carb: 49.4g
- Protein: 9.3g

These Instant Pot noodles are sticky and have an umami flavor. You can use a variety of items as toppings.

Chili Garlic Noodles (Chinese)

Cook time: 3 minutes	Servings: 2

Ingredients

- Soy sauce – ¼ cup
- Brown sugar – 1 tbsp.
- White vinegar – 1 tbsp.

- Chili garlic paste – ½ tbsp.
- Olive oil – ½ tbsp.
- Water – 1 cup
- Uncooked brown rice noodles – 4 oz.
- Raw chicken breasts – ½ lb. cut into small pieces
- Red bell peppers – 1, sliced thinly
- Sesame seeds, green onions, and peanuts for garnish

Method

1. Except for the red pepper, place all the ingredients in the Instant Pot.
2. Cook for 3 minutes on manual and release steam.
3. Open and mix in the red bell pepper and mix gently.
4. Adjust oil or water if necessary.
5. Serve with garnishes.

Nutritional Facts Per Serving

- Calories: 286
- Fat: 5.2g
- Carb: 38.1g
- Protein: 19g

If you love Thai food and want to cook authentic Thai food in your home, then cook this Thai Peanut Noodles recipe.

Thai Peanut Noodles

Cook time: 10 minutes	Servings: 2

Ingredients

- Spaghetti – 4 ounces, broken in half
- Sesame oil – 1 tbsp.
- Garlic – 2 cloves, minced

- Fresh ginger – 1 tbsp. minced
- Red pepper – ¼, thinly sliced
- Honey – 2 tbsps.
- Peanut butter – 2 tbsps.
- Soy sauce – 2 tbsps.
- Vegetable broth – ½ cup
- Rice vinegar – 2 tbsps.
- Sriracha sauce – 2 tsps.
- Chopped cilantro – 1 tbsp.
- Lime juice – ½ tbsp.
- Peanuts for garnish

Method

1. Press Sauté on the IP and add sesame oil.
2. Add sliced peppers, garlic, and ginger. Stir-fry for 2 minutes.
3. Mix together rice vinegar, sriracha sauce, vegetable broth, soy sauce, peanut butter, and honey and add to the IP.
4. Break noodles in half and add to the pot.
5. Make sure they are covered with liquid. Add more liquid if needed.
6. Cover and cook for 5 minutes on High.
7. Serve topped with fresh cilantro, peanuts, and lime juice.

Nutritional Facts Per Serving

- Calories: 514
- Fat: 18g
- Carb: 74g
- Protein: 15g

This noodle dish is called Lo Mein. With an Instant Pot you cook everything in one pot and don't have to drain the noodles.

Lo Mein (Chinese)

Cook time: 10 minutes	Servings: 2

Ingredients

- Garlic – 1 clove, minced
- Sesame oil – ½ tbsp.
- Linguine pasta – 4 oz. broken in half
- Snow peas – ½ cup, trimmed
- Broccoli florets – ½ cup

- Carrots – 1, sliced thin
- Chicken broth - ¾ cup
- Grated ginger – ½ tsp.
- Low sodium soy sauce – 1 tbsp.
- Oyster sauce – ½ tbsp.
- Shaoxing rice wine – ½ tbsp.
- Light brown sugar – ½ tbsp.

Method

1. In the Instant Pot, add the sesame oil and garlic. Press sauté and stir-fry for 2 to 3 minutes.
2. Spread noodles and add vegetables.
3. In a bowl, add the brown sugar, rice wine, oyster sauce, soy sauce, ginger, and broth. Mix well. Taste and adjust seasoning.
4. Pour sauce into the pot.
5. Cover and cook on Manual for 5 minutes on High.
6. Do a quick release and stir the noodles a few times.
7. Stir until the water is gone.
8. Serve.

Nutritional Facts Per Serving

- Calories: 299
- Fat: 4.7g
- Carb: 53.7g
- Protein: 10.1g

This is the easiest and heartiest one pot dinner. Simply add everything in the pot and your dinner is ready after a few minutes.

Chicken Noodle Soup (Chinese)

Cook time: 20 minutes	Servings: 2

Ingredients

- Wheat or rice noodles – 3 oz.
- Chopped greens of your choice – 2 cups
- Eggs for topping
- Toasted sesame oil – ½ tsp.

- Chili oil for serving

Instant Pot ingredients

- Fresh and room temperature boneless skinless chicken breast or thigh – ¾ lb.
- Green onion – 1, chopped and separated
- Garlic – 1 clove, minced
- Ginger – 1 large slice, chopped
- Bay leaf – 1
- Chicken broth – 4 cups
- Shaoxing wine – 1 tbsp.
- Light soy sauce – ½ tbsp.
- Black pepper – 1 pinch
- Salt – 1 pinch

Method

1. Add all the Instant Pot ingredients and white parts of the green onion in the IP.
2. Cover and cook on High for 10 minutes.
3. Do a natural release, remove the meat and shred.
4. Press sauté on the IP.
5. When it starts to boil, add the wheat noodles and cook according to package instructions.
6. Add the eggs and green vegetables 2 minutes before the noodles are ready.
7. Cook until the vegetables are just cooked.
8. Taste and adjust seasoning.
9. Add green part of the green onion and drizzle with sesame oil.
10. Mix and serve topped with Sriracha sauce and chili oil.

Nutritional Facts Per Serving

- Calories: 456
- Fat: 13.9g
- Carb: 29.3g
- Protein: 51.1g

This Chinese noodle recipe uses ramen noodles. They are cooked with soy, sesame, and garlic and turn into a wonderful lunch of noodles.

Chinese Garlic Sesame Noodles

Cook time: 4 minutes	Servings: 2

Ingredients

- Ramen noodles – 2 packages, break in half (discard seasoning packets)
- Water – 2 cups
- Soy sauce – ¼ cup
- Sesame oil – 1 tsp.

- Garlic – 1 tsp.
- Sesame seeds and chives for garnish

Method

1. Add the noodles, water, soy sauce, garlic and oil in the IP.
2. Close the lid and set to manual or 0 minutes.
3. Do a quick release.
4. Stir noodles.
5. Serve garnish with sesame seeds and chives.

Nutritional Facts Per Serving

- Calories: 335
- Fat: 16g
- Carb: 39g
- Protein: 10g

These noodles are delicious and a gluten-free dinner option. This dish is even easier than a stir-fry dish.

Spicy Honey Garlic Noodles (Chinese)

Cook time: 15 minutes	Servings: 2

Ingredients

- Sesame oil – 1/3 tbsp.
- Low sodium soy sauce – 1 1/3 tbsps.
- Garlic – 2 cloves, minced
- Honey – ½ tbsp.
- Chili garlic sauce – 1/3 tbsp.
- Medium-sized chicken breasts – ½, diced
- Water – ½ cup
- Rice noodles – 80 grams
- Sesame seeds for garnish
- Broccoli – 1/3 head, chopped
- Red and yellow bell pepper – 1/3, sliced

Method

1. In the Instant Pot, add the oil, garlic, honey, soy sauce, garlic sauce, water, chicken, and rice noodles.
2. Make sure the noodles are covered with water.
3. Cover and cook on High pressure for 2 minutes.
4. Do a quick release and open the lid.
5. Add the broccoli and bell peppers. Stir to mix.
6. Push the vegetables under the noodles.
7. Cover and let sit for 5 to 10 minutes.
8. Serve.

Nutritional Facts Per Serving

- Calories: 404
- Fat: 15g
- Carb: 40g
- Protein: 26g

CHAPTER 14 VEGETARIAN RECIPES

Make this delicious, crunchy broccoli in just 20 minutes in your Instant Pot or pressure cooker.

Broccoli with Garlic

Cook time: 5 minutes	Servings: 2

Ingredients

- Broccoli – 1 head, cut into 2 cups of florets
- Water – ½ cup
- Garlic – 6 cloves, minced
- Peanut oil – 1 tbsp.

- Rice wine – 1 tbsp.
- Fine sea salt

Method

1. Add ½ cup water in the IP.
2. Place steamer rack into the pressure cooker.
3. Place the broccoli florets onto the steamer rack.
4. Cover and cook on low pressure for 0 minutes.
5. Do a quick release.
6. Place the broccoli in the cold water to stop cooking. Drain and set aside.
7. Remove the water from the IP and towel dry the inner pot.
8. Heat up your pressure cooker on sauté.
9. Add 1 tbsp. oil, and garlic.
10. Stir-fry for 30 seconds. Don't burn.
11. Add the broccoli and 1 tbsp. rice wine.
12. Stir for 30 seconds.
13. Season with salt and serve.

Nutritional Facts Per Serving

- Calories: 147
- Fat: 7.4g
- Carb: 18.4g
- Protein: 5.6g

This is a Sri Lankan budget-friendly, and nutritious vegetable dish. The dish is called mallung or mallum in Sri Lanka. This cabbage dish is made delicious by using spices like turmeric and mustard seeds.

Coconut Cabbage

Cook time: 15 minutes	Servings: 2

Ingredients

- Coconut oil – ½ tbsp.
- Brown onion – ½, sliced
- Salt – ½ tsp.
- Garlic – 1 clove, diced

- Red chili – ¼, sliced
- Yellow mustard seeds – ½ tbsp.
- Mild curry powder – ½ tbsp.
- Turmeric powder – ½ tbsp.
- Cabbage – ½, sliced
- Carrot – ½, sliced
- Lemon juice – 1 tbsp.
- Desiccated unsweetened coconut – ¼ cup
- Olive oil – ½ tbsp.
- Water – ½ cup

Method

1. Press sauté on your Instant Pot.
2. Add oil and onion and half the salt.
3. Sauté for 3 to 4 minutes.
4. Add the spices, chili, and garlic and stir fry for 30 seconds.
5. Add the olive oil, coconut, lime juice, carrots, and cabbage and stir through.
6. Add the water and stir through. Press Cancel.
7. Cover and cook on High pressure for 5 minutes.
8. Do a natural release for 5 minutes
9. Serve.

Nutritional Facts Per Serving

- Calories: 410
- Fat: 31.7g
- Carb: 32.3g
- Protein: 6.9g

This Japanese vegan curry dish is comforting, flavorful, and perfect for weekday dinner.

Vegan Japanese Curry

Cook time: 12 minutes	Servings: 2

Ingredients

- Oil – 1 tsp. divided
- Onion – ¼, sliced

- Garlic – 2 cloves, minced
- Finely chopped ginger – ½ tbsp.
- Flour – ½ tbsp.
- Garam masala – 1 tsp.
- Turmeric 1 pinch
- Chopped carrots – ½ cup
- Potato – ½ cup, cubed
- Chickpeas – 7 oz. drained
- Tomato paste – 1 tsp.
- Vegan Worcestershire sauce - 1 tsp.
- Water – 1 cup
- Salt to taste
- Apple sauce – 1 ½ tbsps.
- Peas – 1 tbsp.
- Rice, pickled ginger, and radish for serving

Method

1. Press sauté on IP.
2. Add oil and add onion to the hot oil.
3. Stir fry until translucent.
4. Add ginger and garlic and mix. Cook for 30 seconds.
5. Move onions to the side and add more oil.
6. Add the flour and mix into the oil.
7. Then mix with the garlic, ginger, and onion. Stir fry for 30 seconds.
8. Add the spices and mix.
9. Add the water, salt, sauces, chickpeas, and vegetables. Mix and remove the stuck flour from the bottom.
10. Cancel sauté.
11. Close and cook on High for 6 to 7 minutes.
12. Once cooked do a natural release.
13. Open the lid and press sauté.

14. Add the peas, and apple sauce and bring to a boil.
15. Taste and adjust spice and salt.
16. Add some pepper and sweetener if needed.
17. Garnish with scallions, radishes and sesame seeds.
18. Serve with rice.

Nutritional Facts Per Serving

- Calories: 209
- Fat: 5g
- Carb: 33g
- Protein: 9g

This is butter chicken, but vegan version. The recipe gives all the butter chicken flavor minus the chicken.

Butter Chickpeas (Indian)

Cook time: 50 minutes	Servings: 2

Ingredients

- Dried chickpeas – 1 cup, soaked overnight, then drained and rinsed
- Oil – 1 tbsp.
- Onion – ½, diced
- Minced garlic – 1 ½ tsp.
- Minced ginger – ½ tsp.

Spices

- Garam masala – ½ tsp.
- Coriander powder – ½ tsp.
- Paprika – ½ tsp.
- Salt – ½ tsp.
- Turmeric – ½ tsp.
- Black pepper – to taste
- Cayenne – to taste
- Ground cumin – to taste
- Tomato sauce – 1
- Water – ¾ cup

Add later

- Green bell pepper – ½, chopped
- Coconut cream – ¼ cup, unsweetened
- Pinch of dried fenugreek leaves
- Cilantro for garnish

Method

1. Press the sauté button.
2. Add the oil and heat.
3. Add the onion and stir fry for 6 to 7 minutes.

4. Add the spices, ginger, and garlic and add the tomato sauce, chickpeas, and water.
5. Cover with the lid and cook on High for 35 minutes.
6. Do a natural pressure release.
7. Add fenugreek leaves, cream, and bell pepper. Mix well.
8. Garnish with cilantro and serve.

Nutritional Facts Per Serving

- Calories: 470
- Fat: 13.3g
- Carb: 70.8g
- Protein: 21.4g

This Indian vegetable biryani is flavorful, aromatic, and tasty.

Vegetable Biryani

Cook time: 15 minutes	Servings: 2

Ingredients

- Basmati rice – ½ cup (soaked for 15 minutes, then drained)
- Oil – 1 tbsp.

Whole Spice

- Cardamom pods – 2
- Whole cloves – 2
- Bay leaf – 1
- Cinnamon stick – ¼

- Cumin seeds –¼ tsp.
- Fennel seeds – ¼ tsp.
- Onion – ½, thinly sliced
- Minced garlic – 1 tsp.
- Minced ginger – ½ tsp.

Ground spices

- Salt – ½ tsp.
- Coriander powder – ½ tsp.
- Paprika – ½ tsp.
- Garam masala – to taste
- Black pepper – to taste
- Cayenne – to taste
- Ground cumin - to taste
- Turmeric – to taste

Vegetables

- Bell pepper – ½, cut into strips
- Baby carrots – ½ cup
- Frozen veggies – ½ cup
- Gold potatoes – ¼ pound, cut in half
- Water – ½ cup
- Cilantro leaves, mint leaves
- Ghee coated cashews and raisins

Method

1. Press Sauté and add the oil to the pot.
2. Add the whole spice to the hot oil and stir.
3. Once the cumin is brown, add the onions, and stir-fry for 5 to 7 minutes.
4. Add the ground spices, ginger, garlic, and stir.
5. Add the vegetables, rice, and water and stir.

6. Cover and cook 6 minutes at High.
7. Do a natural release.
8. Open and add mint, cilantro, cashews, and raisins.
9. Mix and serve.

Nutritional Facts Per Serving

- Calories: 305
- Fat: 8.3g
- Carb: 52.8g
- Protein: 5.9g

This Indian Kidney bean curry dish has a thick masala gravy and is full of flavors.

Kidney Bean Curry

Cook time: 45 minutes	Servings: 2

Ingredients

- Dried kidney beans – 1 cup, soaked overnight
- Onion – ½, roughly chopped
- Serrano pepper or green chili – ¼
- Oil – 1 ½ tbsp.
- Cumin seeds – ½ tsp.
- Bay leaf – 1
- Minced garlic – 1 tsp.

- Minced ginger – 1 tsp.

Spices

- Salt – 1 tsp.
- Coriander powder – ½ tsp.
- Garam masala – ½ tsp.
- Paprika – ½ tsp.
- Black pepper – ¼ tsp.
- Turmeric – ½ tsp.
- Cayenne – 1 pinch
- Fresh tomato puree – 1 cup
- Water – 1 cup
- Cilantro for garnish

Method

1. Blend the serrano pepper and onion in a food processor until smooth. Set aside.
2. Press the Sauté on the IP.
3. Add the oil and heat.
4. Add the cumin seeds and heat until browned.
5. Add the blended serrano pepper and onion and stir fry for 8 to 10 minutes.
6. Add the spices, ginger, garlic, and bay leaf.
7. Add the tomato puree and stir fry for 5 minutes.
8. Add the water and kidney beans.
9. Cover with the lid and cook on High for 30 minutes.
10. Do a natural release.
11. Garnish with cilantro and serve.

Nutritional Facts Per Serving

- Calories: 455
- Fat: 15g
- Carb: 60.5g
- Protein: 21.3g

This Indian popular vegetable korma is a part of Mughal cuisine. This dish is made with cream, nuts, and dried fruits.

Vegetable Korma

Cook time: 20 minutes	Servings: 2

Ingredients

Onion tomato sauce

- Onion – ½, roughly chopped
- Garlic – 2 cloves, chopped
- Ginger – 1 inch, chopped
- Tomato -1/2 chopped
- Serrano pepper or green chili – ¼ tsp.

Cashew Sauce

- Water – ½ cup

- Cashews – ¼ cup
- Heavy cream – 2 tbsps.
- Ghee – 1 ½ tbsps.
- Cashews – 2 tbsps.
- Golden raisins - 2 tbsps.
- Cumin seeds – ¼ tsp.

Spices

- Paprika – 1 tsp.
- Salt – 1/2 tsp.
- Coriander powder – ½ tsp.
- Turmeric powder – ¼ tsp.
- Garam masala – ¼ tsp.
- Cayenne – a pinch
- Ground cardamom - a pinch
- Chopped potato – 1 cup
- Water – ½ cup
- Chopped vegetables – 2 cups (broccoli, green beans, peas, carrots)
- Dried fenugreek leaves – ¼ tsp.
- Cilantro for garnish

Method

1. To make the tomato sauce: in a blender, add the serrano, tomato, ginger, garlic, and onion and blend until smooth. Set aside.
2. Prepare the cashew sauce: blend heavy cream, cashews, and water until smooth. Set aside.
3. Press the sauté on the Instant Pot.
4. Add the ghee, golden raisins and cashews.
5. Stir fry until the cashews turn golden.

6. Remove the raisins and cashews from the pot and set aside.
7. Add the cumin seeds to the pot.
8. Once they start to brown, add the tomato and onion mixture.
9. Stir fry for 7 to 8 minutes.
10. Add all the remaining spices and the potatoes. Mix well.
11. Add the water and cover.
12. Cook on High for 5 minutes.
13. Do a quick release.
14. Add the remaining chopped vegetables.
15. Cover and cook on High for 2 minutes.
16. Do a quick release.
17. Stir in fenugreek leaves, and cashew sauce.
18. Garnish with ghee-coated raisins, and cashews and cilantro.
19. Serve.

Nutritional Facts Per Serving

- Calories: 380
- Fat: 24.6g
- Carb: 31.1g
- Protein: 8.6g

This Indian recipe is called Aloo baingan masala. It is made with spiced eggplant and potatoes.

Spiced Potato and Eggplant

Cook time: 5 minutes	Servings: 2

Ingredients

- Oil – ½ tbsp.
- Cumin seeds – ¼ tsp.
- Serrano pepper – ½, minced
- Golden potatoes – ½ pound, chopped
- Eggplant – ¾ pound, chopped
- Water – ¼ cup
- Onion masala – ¼ cup (recipe below)
- Salt – ½ tsp.
- Garam masala – ¼ tsp.

- Cilantro for garnish

Method

1. Press the Sauté and add oil.
2. Add serrano pepper and cumin seeds to the hot oil.
3. Add the remaining ingredients once the cumin seeds are brown.
4. Cover with the lid and cook on High for 4 minutes.
5. Do a quick release.
6. Mix well.
7. Garnish and serve.

Nutritional Facts Per Serving

- Calories: 155
- Fat: 3.8g
- Carb: 29.5g
- Protein: 3.4g

This Indian Punjabi Dal recipe is made with only a few ingredients, but full of flavor.

Langar Dal

Cook time: 30 minutes	Servings: 2

Ingredients

- Ghee – 2 tbsps. divided
- Cumin seeds – ½ tsp.

- Urad dal – ½ cup, soaked in cold water overnight
- Chana dal – 2 tbsp.
- Water – 2 cups
- Onion masala – ½ cup
- Salt – ¾ tsp.
- Garam masala – ¾ tsp.
- Cayenne – ¼ tsp.
- Cilantro and heavy cream for garnish

Method

1. Press the sauté button on the IP.
2. Add 1 tbsp. ghee to the pot and add cumin seeds to the melted ghee.
3. Add the remaining ingredients to the pot when the cumin seeds are brown.
4. Cover and cook on High for 30 minutes.
5. Do a natural release.
6. Stir in the remaining ingredients.
7. Garnish with the cilantro and heavy cream and serve.

Nutritional Facts Per Serving

- Calories: 338
- Fat: 13.6g
- Carb: 39.1g
- Protein: 16g

This Indian egg biryani is flavorful, delicious and easy to make.

Egg Biryani

Cook time: 20 minutes	Servings: 2

Ingredients

- Basmati rice – 1 cup, soaked for 15 minutes
- Ghee – 2 tbsps.

Whole spices

- Cardamom pods – 5
- Whole cloves – 4
- Bay leaf – 2
- Cinnamon stick – ½ inch
- Cumin seeds – ½ tsp.
- Fennel seeds – ½ tsp.
- Oil – 2 tbsps.
- Onion – 1, thinly sliced
- Minced garlic – 2 tsps.

- Minced ginger – 1 tsp.
- Tomato – 1, diced

Ground spices

- Salt – 1 ½ tsp.
- Coriander powder – 1 tsp.
- Paprika – 1 tsp.
- Garam masala – ½ tsp.
- Black pepper – ¼ tsp.
- Cayenne – ¼ tsp.
- Ground cumin – ¼ tsp.
- Turmeric – ¼ tsp.
- Water – 1 cup
- Eggs - 6
- Cilantro leaves, chopped
- Mint leaves, chopped
- Ghee coated raisins and cashews

Method

1. Press the sauté button and add the oil to the Instant Pot.
2. Add the whole spices and stir.
3. Add the onions once the cumin seeds are brown.
4. Stir-fry for 5 to 7 minutes.
5. Add the ground spices, ginger, garlic, and tomato.
6. Cook for 2 to 3 minutes.
7. Add the rice and water.
8. Then place a steamer basket on top of the rice.
9. Place the eggs in the steamer basket.
10. Cover and cook on High for 10 minutes.
11. Do a quick release.
12. Remove the eggs, cool and peel them. You can stir fry the eggs if necessary.

13. Place the peeled eggs back into the rice and mix well.
14. Garnish with ghee coated cashews and raisins, mint, and cilantro.
15. Serve.

Nutritional Facts Per Serving

- Calories: 835
- Fat: 41.9g
- Carb: 91.4g
- Protein: 25.7g

CHAPTER 15 DESSERTS AND SNACKS

This is Filipino rice pudding. This dish is sweet, delicious and you will enjoy making this recipe. The fresh mango slices and caramel topping makes this recipe delicious.

Filipino Sweet Rice Cake

Cook time: 75 + minutes	Servings: 4

Ingredients

- Asian sweet rice – 1 ½ cups
- Coconut milk – 2 cans
- White sugar – ½ cup
- Light brown sugar – ½ cup
- Vanilla – 1 tsp.
- Water – 3 cups

Caramel topping sauce

Ingredients

- Brown sugar – 1 cup
- Half-and-half – ½ cup
- Butter – 4 tbsp.
- Pinch salt
- Vanilla extract – 1 tbsp.

Method

1. Fill your pot with 3 cups of water.
2. In a bowl, add rice and sugar. Mix well.
3. Add the vanilla and coconut milk, mix well and cover with aluminum foil.
4. Add a wire stand to your pot. Make sure the stand is high enough so the bowl will not touch the water at the bottom.
5. Cover and press Manual for 75 minutes.
6. Do a natural release and cool for 15 minutes.
7. Open the pot and check the middle.
8. If it needs more time, then cover and let sit for 10 minutes more.

9. Remove when the rice is cooked completely.
10. Add a caramel topping and serve.
11. Caramel topping: mix all the ingredients in a pan over medium heat.
12. Cook and whisk until dark, about 5 to 7 minutes.

Nutritional Facts Per Serving

- Calories: 573
- Fat: 28.6g
- Carb: 82.4g
- Protein: 3.9g

This is a Filipino Leche Flan dish. This dish is made only on special occasions such as Thanksgiving, or Christmas. Use an oven safe bowl when making this recipe.

Filipino Leche Flan

Cook time: 16 to 35 minutes	Servings: 5

Ingredients

- Egg yolks – 10
- Condensed milk – 1 can

- Evaporated milk – 1 can
- Sugar – ½ cup
- Vanilla – 1 tsp.
- Water – 2 cups
- Caramel

Method

1. Whisk the egg yolks, but do not over mix.
2. Gently add both the milks. Mix well.
3. Mix in sugar and vanilla. Do not over mix.
4. Add the water in the pressure cooker and add the trivet.
5. Pour in caramel in 2 bowls so the bottom is covered.
6. Add the mixture in two bowls evenly.
7. Cover each bowl with foil. Tap to release any extra bubbles.
8. Gently place the bowl on the trivet.
9. Cover and cook on Manual for 16 minutes.
10. Then do a natural release for 10 minutes.
11. Remove and check with a toothpick.
12. If they are still not cooked, then repeat the cooking time.
13. When cooked, cool and place in the refrigerator overnight.
14. Serve.

Nutritional Facts Per Serving

- Calories: 290
- Fat: 23g
- Carb: 4g
- Protein: 16g

This is a very easy Instant Pot pudding recipe. This soybean pudding is drizzled with sweet ginger syrup.

Tofu Pudding (Singaporean)

Cook time: 15 minutes	Servings: 4

Ingredients

Soy milk

- Dry soybeans – 1 cup
- Cold water for soaking – 3 cups
- Cold water – 6 cups
- Salt - 1 pinch

Tofu pudding

- Agar-agar powder – 1 tsp.
- Granulated sugar – 2 to 3 tbsp.

Ginger syrup

- Rock sugar – 200 grams
- Water – 1 cup
- Brown sugar – 3 tbsps.
- Ginger – 3 tbsps. crushed

Method

1. Soak the soybeans: in the pressure cooker, add 3 cups cold water and 1 cup dried soybeans.
2. Close the lid and cook at High pressure for 0 minute.
3. Do a 30-minute natural release. Discard the soaking water and rinse the beans under cold water.
4. To make the pudding: in a blender, blend the soybeans with 2 cups of water until smooth.
5. To cook: place the steamer basket in the Instant Pot.
6. Add 4 cups of cold water and 1 pinch of salt.
7. Add the soybean mixture.
8. Close and pressure cook on High for 5 minutes.
9. Then do a 25-minute natural release.
10. Syrup: add the ingredients in a saucepan and bring to a simmer over medium heat.
11. Stir until sugar melts. Lower heat and simmer for 2 minutes more.
12. Discard ginger and simmer until thickens, about 5 to 10 minutes more.
13. Remove from the heat and cool the syrup.
14. Strain the soy milk.
15. Add agar-agar power to a saucepan and add the soy milk.
16. Stir and bring the mixture to a simmer and mix well.
17. Add granulated sugar to sweeten the pudding.
18. Cool and serve.

Nutritional Facts Per Serving

- Calories: 402
- Fat: 6.3g
- Carb: 78.9g
- Protein: 11.6g

This Sri Lankan dish is called Watalappan in Sri Lanka. This dish is made with spices such as nutmeg and cardamom and sweetened with traditional Kitul jiggery.

Watalappan (Sri Lankan)

Cook time: 15 minutes	Servings: 2

Ingredients

- Eggs – 2

- Brown molasses sugar or kitul jiggery – 125 gramss (shaved with a knife)
- Canned coconut milk – ½ cup
- Cardamom powder –1 pinch
- Salt – 1 pinch
- Roasted cashews for garnish

Method

1. Heat a pan on medium heat.
2. Add 2 tbsps. water and shaved jiggery.
3. Melt until dissolved. Remove from heat and cool.
4. Whisk in the coconut milk.
5. In another bowl, whisk the eggs, with cardamom and salt.
6. Add the coconut milk mixture to the eggs and whisk to combine. Don't make it frothy.
7. Strain the mixture and pour into two ramekins or one large dish.
8. Add 2 cups of water in the Instant Pot and place the steaming insert.
9. Place the ramekins on the insert.
10. Close and seam for 15 minutes.
11. Release pressure and remove the ramekins.
12. Cool and serve.

Nutritional Facts Per Serving

- Calories: 439
- Fat: 19.6g
- Carb: 64g
- Protein: 7.8g

Called Ji Dan Gao, this Instant Pot Chinese Matcha Sponge Cake is lightly flavored and spongy.

Chinese Sponge Cake

Cook time: 20 minutes	Servings: 5

Ingredients

- Eggs – 2
- Sugar – 120 grams
- Matcha powder – 1 tbsp.

- Sprite – 100 ml
- Cake flour – 120 gram

Method

1. In a bowl, place the matcha, sugar, and eggs.
2. Beat with a hand mixer for 1 minute on medium speed.
3. Then increase the speed and beat on high for 20 minutes to make it as light as the sponge.
4. The batter will be double in volume.
5. Lower the speed to low and gradually add in soda drink and flour.
6. Just mix so there is no lump remains.
7. Prepare a 5 to 6-inch container and line with parchment paper.
8. Pour batter into the prepared container and break up any bubbles.
9. Place the trivet in the Pot.
10. Add 3 cups of water.
11. Gently place the cake container on top of the trivet.
12. Close and press Steam.
13. Cook on High for 20 minutes.
14. Do a natural release.
15. Remove and cool.
16. Serve.

Nutritional Facts Per Serving

- Calories: 216
- Fat: 2.2g
- Carb: 44.7g
- Protein: 5g

This traditional Chinese rice pudding dessert recipe is made with nuts, fruits, and seeds.

Rice Pudding (Ba Bao Fan)

Cook time: 1 hour 6 minutes	Servings: 4

Ingredients

- Glutinous rice – 1 cup, rinsed and drained
- Water – 2 cups, and more as needed
- Brown sugar – 1 ½ tbsps.
- Butter – 1 tbsp.
- Red bean paste – 1 cup

Dried fruits

- Dried candied mango – 2 slices
- Golden raisins – 1 tbsp.
- Goji berries – 1 tbsp.
- Dried cranberries – 1 tbsp.
- Dried longan – 2 tbsp.
- Chinese red dates – 4
- Chinese black dates – 4

Soak all the dried fruits in warm water for 30 minutes.

Syrup

- Sugar – ¼ cup
- Water – ½ cup

Dried fruit for the syrup

- Golden raisin – 1 tbsp.
- Dried cranberries – 1 tbsp.

Serve with

- Condensed milk

Method

1. Add the water in the IP.
2. Put the trivet in.
3. Add the rice in a stainless-steel bowl and add enough water to cover the rice. Mix to make sure all the rice is submerged in water.
4. Place the bowl on top of the trivet.
5. Close the lid and cook on High pressure for 15 minutes.
6. Do a natural release.

7. Open the lid and stir in the butter and brown sugar.
8. To assemble: add more 2 cups more water in the IP.
9. Add the soaked dried fruit and red bean paste with the rice pudding.
10. If you want to decorate then arrange rice, dried fruit, and red bean paste in layers.
11. Smooth with a rubber spatula.
12. Cover and press Steamer.
13. Cook for 30 minutes.
14. Prepare the syrup: in a saucepan, place dried fruits, sugar and water.
15. Cook on medium heat until the mixture gets a syrup consistency.
16. Serve the rice pudding with syrup and condensed milk.

Nutritional Facts Per Serving

- Calories: 276
- Fat: 3.4g
- Carb: 58g
- Protein: 4.5g

Making this traditional Chinese Lunar New Year cake is easy.

Chinese New Year Cake (Kue Bakul)

Cook time: 1 hour 10 minutes	Servings: 7x 3 inch round cake

Ingredients

- Glutinous rice flour – 300 grams
- Water – 300 mls
- White sugar – 300 grams
- Dark brown sugar – 100 grams
- Long sheet of banana leaves – 4 to 5 (blanch in hot boiling water for 5 minutes, then pat dry)

Method

1. Cut the banana leaves into 7-inch width and about 7 to 8-inch length. Arrange them on the bottom of a 7 X 3 inch round cake pan so they cover the bottom and all the sides.
2. In a saucepan, place the water and sugar and bring to a boil to melt the sugar.
3. Remove from the heat and cool completely.
4. Gradually add the flour into the sugar mixture.
5. Stir to mix until smooth.
6. Pour the batter into the prepared aluminum pan and cover with aluminum foil.
7. Pour 1 cup of water into the IP.
8. Set the trivet.
9. Place the cake pan on top of the trivet.
10. Cover and cook on High for 45 minutes.
11. Do a natural release.
12. Remove and cool for 24 hours to harden.
13. Serve.

Nutritional Facts for the Entire Recipe

- Calories: 2595
- Fat: 2g
- Carb: 639.9g
- Protein: 21.4g

This silky-smooth egg custard recipe takes only 4 ingredients and 4 steps to make.

Chinese Egg Custard

Cook time: 16 minutes	Servings: 4 to 5

Ingredients

- Eggs – 3, beaten
- Whole milk – 1 ½ cup, divided
- A pinch of salt
- Sugar – 4 tbsps. or 5 tbsps. for more sweetness

Method

1. In a pan, add sugar, 1 cup milk, and a pinch of salt.

2. Whisk and heat until sugar melts.
3. Add the remaining milk and mix.
4. The mixture should cool to touch.
5. Slowly pour the milk mixture into the beaten eggs and whisk.
6. Then strain the milk-egg mixture.
7. Pour the mixture into 4 to 5 ramekins.
8. Cover the ramekins tightly with foil.
9. Add 1 cup of water in the Instant Pot.
10. Place a trivet in the IP.
11. And gently place the ramekins on the trivet.
12. Cover and cook on Low for 0 minutes.
13. Do a natural release.
14. Open and serve.

Nutritional Facts Per Serving

- Calories: 119
- Fat: 4g
- Carb: 13g
- Protein: 5g

This Asian popsicle recipe is made with just 5 ingredients. They are full of sweet and nutty beans and are delicious.

Adzuki Beans Coconut Popsicles

Cook time: 55 minutes	Servings: 10 Ice Pops

Ingredients

- Adzuki beans – 240 grams
- Cold running water – 5 cups

- Brown rock sugar in pieces – 2 ½ to 3 ½ pieces (70 grams each)
- Coconut milk – ¾ cup, plus 1 tbsp.
- Cornstarch – 1 ½ tbsps. plus 2 tbsps. water

Method

1. Rinse the beans under cold water and drain.
2. Place 5 cups of water and beans in the pressure cooker.
3. Close and cook on High for 20 minutes.
4. Do a natural release for 15 minutes.
5. Open the lid and press sauté.
6. Add the brown rock sugar.
7. Stir and boil for 10 minutes or until sugar melts.
8. Mix in the coconut milk and adjust the sweetness.
9. Mix the cornstarch with water.
10. Gradually add to the Instant Pot mixture.
11. Turn off the heat.
12. Cool the mixture completely.
13. And fill the popsicle molds.
14. Freeze for 6 hours and serve.

Nutritional Facts Per Serving

- Calories: 144
- Fat: 5.8g
- Carb: 24.8g
- Protein: 1g

This is a popular Taiwanese street food made with 6 ingredients. Serve with yummy sauce.

Taiwanese Corn on the Cob

Cook time: 20 minutes	Servings: 2 to 4

Ingredients

- Corn on the cob – 4 ears

Sauce

- Light soy sauce – 3 tbsps.
- Shacha sauce – 2 tbsps.

- Sugar – 1 tbsp.
- Garlic powder – 1 tsp.
- Sesame oil – ¼ tsp.

Method

1. Add 1 cup water into the pressure cooker.
2. Place a trivet in the pressure cooker.
3. Place 4 ears of corn on the cob onto the trivet.
4. Close and cook on High for 1 to 2 minutes.
5. Do a quick release.
6. Open the lid and remove.
7. Preheat the oven to 450F.
8. In a bowl, mix all the sauce ingredients.
9. Brush the sauce all over the corn on the cob.
10. Place them in a baking rack.
11. Bake for 5 to 10 minutes.
12. Serve.

Nutritional Facts Per Serving

- Calories: 85
- Fat: 0.8g
- Carb: 19.1g
- Protein: 3.3g

CHAPTER 16 KETO ASIAN RECIPES

This is a low-carb, Ketogenic, delicious chicken dish cooked in less than 30 minutes. The secret of this dish is the use of a lot of tomato and ginger.

Keto Pakistani Karachi Chicken

Cook time: 15 minutes	Servings: 2

Ingredients

- Oil – 1 tbsp.

- Grated ginger – 2 tbsp.
- Boneless, skinless chicken thighs – ½ lb. cut into pieces
- Canned diced tomatoes – ¾ cup
- Ground cumin – 1/3 tsp.
- Garam masala – 1/3 tsp.
- Cayenne – 1/3 tsp.
- Salt – 1/3 tsp.

For finishing

- Chopped cilantro or parsley – 1 tsp.
- Lemon juice – 1 tbsp.
- Garam masala – 1/3 tsp.
- Fresh ginger to taste, thinly cut

Method

1. Add oil to a hot Instant Pot.
2. Add the thinly sliced ginger and cook for 2 to 3 minutes.
3. Add the spices, tomatoes, and chicken and stir well.
4. Close the lid and cook on High for 5 minutes.
5. When done, do a natural release for 10 minutes.
6. Garnish with finishing ingredients and serve.

Nutritional Facts Per Serving

- Calories: 202
- Fat: 9g
- Carb: 5g
- Protein: 22g

Traditionally cooked in a tandoor (oven), this is now can be cooked using an Instant Pot. This dish is succulent, moist and a favorite for the whole family.

Pakistani Tandoori Chicken

Cook time: 30 minutes	Servings: 2

Ingredients

- Chicken drumsticks – 8 (1 lb.), skinned and dried with a paper towel
- Plain yogurt – ¼ cup
- Ginger – ¼ tbsp. grated
- Garlic – ¼ tbsp. minced
- Kashmiri red chili powder – ½ tbsp.

- Turmeric – ¼ tsp.
- Garam masala – ½ tsp.
- Salt – 1 tsp.
- Lemon juice – ½ tbsp.
- Oil – ½ tbsp.
- Water – 1 cup

Method

1. In a bowl, add the oil, lemon juice, salt, garam masala, turmeric, chili powder, garlic, ginger, and yogurt. Mix well.
2. Make 2 to 3 slits on each chicken piece and coat with marinade. Marinate up to 24 hours in the refrigerator and remove chicken 30 minutes before cooking.
3. Add 1 cup water to the Instant Pot and grease the trivet with cooking oil. place the trivet in the IP.
4. Arrange the marinated chicken pieces on the trivet.
5. Close and cook on High for 15 minutes, then do a natural release.
6. Enjoy tandoori chicken with low-carb chutney and lime wedges.

Nutritional Facts Per Serving

- Calories: 331
- Fat: 11g
- Carb: 3g
- Protein: 50g

This Instant Pot chicken curry is made using whole spices and a simple tomato-onion gravy. The secret of this recipe is you need to sauté both onions and tomatoes for a bit longer, about 4 minutes each.

Chicken Curry (Indian)

Cook time: 20 minutes	Servings: 2

Ingredients

- Chicken – ½ pound, cut into bite-size pieces
- Ghee or oil – 1 ½ tbsp.
- Green chili pepper – 1, small chopped
- Ginger – ½ inch, chopped
- Garlic – 2 cloves, chopped
- Onion – ½, chopped
- Medium tomato – 1, chopped

- Water – ½ cup
- Lemon juice – ½ tbsp.
- Cilantro – 1 tbsp. for garnish

Whole spices

- Black cardamom – 1
- Bay leaf – 1
- Cloves – 3
- Black peppercorns – 3
- Cumin seeds – ¼ tsp.

Spices

- Coriander powder – 1 tsp.
- Cayenne or red chili powder – ¼ tsp.
- Garam masala – ¼ tsp.
- Ground turmeric – a pinch
- Salt – ½ tsp.

Method

1. Press Sauté and add the oil to the Instant Pot.
2. Add whole spices and sauté for 30 seconds.
3. Add the garlic, ginger, onion, and green chili and sauté for 4 minutes. Stirring continuously.
4. Add the spices and chopped tomato. Cook and stir for 4 more minutes.
5. Add the chicken and sauté for 2 minutes. Add water and stir to mix.
6. Cover and cook on manual for 5 minutes on High pressure.
7. Do a quick release. Open and stir in the lemon juice.
8. Garnish with cilantro and serve.

Nutritional Facts Per Serving

- Calories: 386
- Fat: 30g
- Carb: 8g
- Protein: 19g

Chicken Kadai or chicken Karachi is a spicy curry recipe made with fresh ginger and fragrant spices. It is a popular Pakistani and North Indian curry dish.

Chicken Karachi

Cook time: 20 minutes	Servings: 2

Ingredients

- Olive oil – 1 ½ tbsps.
- Yellow onion – ½, diced
- Ginger – 1 tbsp. diced
- Garlic – 1 tbsp. minced
- Boneless, skinless chicken thighs – ¾ pound, cut into pieces
- Canned diced tomatoes – ¾ cup
- Ground cumin – ½ tsp.
- Ground coriander – ½ tsp.
- Garam masala – ½ tsp.

- Kashmiri red chili powder – ½ tbsp.
- Ground turmeric – a pinch
- Kosher salt – ¾ tsp.

Garnish

- Chopped cilantro to taste
- Ginger to taste, sliced

Method

1. Press sauté on your Instant Pot and add oil to heat.
2. Add garlic, ginger, and onion and cook for 2 to 3 minutes or until onions are translucent.
3. Add the ground turmeric, red chili powder, garam masala, ground coriander, ground cumin, tomato, chicken and salt. Mix well.
4. Close the pot and cook on Manual for 5 minutes on High pressure.
5. Do a quick pressure release when cooked. Then release all remaining pressure and open the lid.
6. Press Sauté mode and cook for 5 minutes to thicken the curry.
7. Garnish with ginger and cilantro.
8. Serve hot with cauliflower rice or almond bread.

Nutritional Facts Per Serving

- Calories: 347
- Fat: 18g
- Carb: 11g
- Protein: 34g

This Indonesian Oxtail soup or Sup Buntut is delicious and low-carb. Just like any other Asian dish, this soup has sweet and salty flavors.

Indonesian Oxtail Soup (Sup Buntut)

Cook time: 1 hour 10 minutes	Servings: 2

Ingredients

Spice Paste

- Shallots – 4

- Garlic – 2 cloves
- Young ginger – ¼ inch
- Nutmeg – ¼ tsp.

Soup

- Oxtail pieces – 300 grams
- Carrots – 1, sliced
- Cinnamon – ½ stick
- Whole cloves – 2
- Tomatoes – 1, sliced
- Oil – ½ tbsp.
- Salt – ½ tsp.
- Sugar substitute – 1 tsp.
- Ground white pepper – ½ tsp.
- Fish sauce – ½ tbsp.
- Fried shallots for garnishing
- Coriander leaves for garnishing
- Water – 2 cups

Method

1. Place the oxtail in the IP and add water.
2. Close and cook on Manual for 50 minutes on High pressure.
3. Release pressure naturally.
4. Skim off the layer of oil
5. Drain the oxtail and stock.
6. Clean the inner pot and press sauté.
7. Add oil and sauté the cloves, cinnamon and spice paste ingredients for 5 minutes.
8. Add the stock and oxtail back into the pot.
9. Add the pepper, sugar substitute, salt, carrot, and fish sauce.

10. Close and on Manual, cook for 10 minutes on High pressure.
11. Do a quick release.
12. Skim off any remaining scum or oil.
13. Add the tomato and mix.
14. Ladle soup into bowls and garnish with fresh red chilies, coriander, and shallots.

Nutritional Facts Per Serving

- Calories: 351
- Fat: 24.9g
- Carb: 10.8g
- Protein: 23g

This pork butt recipe is delicious and fatty. You will get a lot of oil when you have done the cooking. Use a spoon to drain the fat if you don't like too much fat.

Filipino Pork Adobo

Cook time: 30 minutes	Servings: 2

Ingredients

- Pork butt – 1 lb. cut into large cubes
- Soy sauce – 1 tbsp.
- Apple cider vinegar – 1 tbsp.
- Minced garlic – 1 tbsp.
- Bay leaves – 1
- Black pepper to taste
- Oregano – ¼ tsp.
- Coconut oil to taste

Method

1. Sauté pork with oil for 5 minutes in the Instant Pot.
2. Add all the other ingredients and mix.
3. Cancel sauté and press Meat.
4. Cook for 25 minutes
5. Do a natural release for 10 minutes, then do a quick release.
6. Serve.

Nutritional Facts Per Serving

- Calories: 348
- Fat: 22g
- Carb: 2.6g
- Protein: 32.8g

This is a juicy and tender Instant Pot pork chop recipe from Hong Kong. This recipe is made with a sweet-savory umami sauce.

Pork Chops

Cook time: 15 minutes	Servings: 2

Ingredients

- Boneless pork chops – 2 (1.25 inch thick) tenderize the pork chops with a knife
- Small onion – ½ sliced
- Olive oil – ½ tbsp.
- Balsamic vinegar – ½ tbsp.
- Worcestershire sauce – ½ tbsp.
- Liquid aminos – ½ tbsp.
- Erythritol – ½ tsp.
- Unsalted chicken stock – ½ cup
- Cornstarch – 1 tsp. plus 1 tbsp. water mixed
- Kosher salt

Marinade

- Liquid aminos – ½ tbsp.
- Shaoxing wine – ½ tbsp.
- Salt to taste
- Erythritol to taste
- Ground white pepper to taste
- Sesame oil – ¼ tsp.

Method

1. Mix the chops with marinade ingredients and marinate for 20 minutes.
2. Press Sauté and add oil to the pot.
3. Brown the pork chops on both sides. Remove and set aside.
4. Add sliced onions and sauté. Add salt and pepper to taste.
5. Cook for 1 minute.
6. Add the vinegar and deglaze the pot.

7. Add the chicken stock, liquid aminos, Worcestershire sauce, and erythritol. Mix well. Taste and adjust seasoning.
8. Add the pork chops and cook on High pressure for 1 minute. Do a natural release for 10 minutes. Remove pork chops and set aside.
9. Press Sauté. Taste and adjust seasoning.
10. Mix the cornstarch and water.
11. Then mix it into the onion sauce one-third at a time.
12. Serve the pork chops.

Nutritional Facts Per Serving

- Calories: 294
- Fat: 13g
- Carb: 9g
- Protein: 31g

This fish curry is an Instant Pot version of traditional fish curry from the southern part of India. You can add more heat by adding more serrano chilies or jalapeno.

Indian Fish Curry

Cook time: 10 minutes	Servings: 2

Ingredients

- Coconut oil – 1 tbsp.
- Curry leaves – 5

- Onion – ½ cup, chopped
- Garlic – ½ tbsp. chopped
- Ginger – ½ tbsp. chopped
- Jalapeno or serrano chili pepper – 1, chopped
- Tomato – ½ cup, chopped
- Ground coriander – ½ tsp.
- Ground cumin – 1 pinch
- Turmeric – ¼ tsp.
- Black pepper – ¼ tsp.
- Salt – ½ tsp.
- Water – for deglazing
- Canned coconut milk – ½ cup
- Fish fillets – ¾ lb. cut into 2-inch pieces
- Lime juice – ½ tsp.
- Fresh cilantro leaves and tomato slices for garnish

Method

1. Press Sauté on your IP.
2. Add coconut oil and heat up.
3. Add curry leaves and stir fry for 20 seconds.
4. Add green chilies, ginger, garlic, and onions to the IP.
5. Stir fry until onions are translucent.
6. Add tomatoes and sauté until the tomatoes start to break down and release juice.
7. Add the salt, black pepper, turmeric, cumin, and coriander.
8. Sauté for 30 seconds, or until fragrant.
9. Deglaze with a little water.
10. Stir in coconut milk.
11. Add the fish pieces.
12. Make sure the milk goes under the fish pieces.
13. Close and cook pressure cook for 2 minutes.

14. Do a quick release and open the lid.
15. Add the lime juice and gently mix.
16. Serve the fish and gravy in bowls.
17. Garnish with fresh tomato slices, and chopped cilantro.

Nutritional Facts Per Serving

- Calories: 190
- Fat: 11g
- Carb: 6g
- Protein: 16g

This Korean savory pork dish is flavorful. Cooked in a pressure cooker, it is deliciously tender.

Korean Spicy Pork (Dae Ji Bulgogi)

Cook time: 30 minutes	Servings: 2

Ingredients for the marinating and cooking

- Pork shoulder – ½ lb. cut into ½ inch slices
- Onion – ½, sliced thin
- Minced ginger – ½ tbsp.

- Minced garlic – ½ tbsp.
- Liquid aminos – ½ tbsp.
- Rice wine – ½ tbsp.
- Sesame oil – ½ tbsp.
- Splenda – 1 packet
- Gochujang – 1 tbsp.
- Cayenne or gochugaru – ½ tsp.
- Water – 1/6 cup

For the finishing

- Onion – ½, thinly sliced
- Sesame seeds – ½ tbsp.
- Sliced green onions – 4

Method

1. Mix up all the cooking and marinade ingredients in the IP.
2. Allow to sit for 1 hour to a day.
3. Cook on high pressure for 20 minutes.
4. Do a natural pressure release and open the lid.
5. Heat up a pan and add the pork cubes and sliced onion in it.
6. Allow to get very hot and add ½ cup of the sauce from the IP.
7. The sauce will caramelize and mix well with the pork.
8. Once the sauce has evaporated, sprinkle with green onions and sesame seeds.
9. Serve.

Nutritional Facts Per Serving

- Calories: 189

- Fat: 9g
- Carb: 9g
- Protein: 15g

This Taiwanese Beef stew dish is flavorful, tender and delicious.

Taiwanese Beef Stew

Cook time: 45 minutes	Servings: 2

Ingredients for aromatics

- Medium yellow onion – ½, chopped
- Large garlic cloves – 5, chopped
- Finely chopped ginger – 1 tbsp.

- Red chili pepper or jalapeno – ½, chopped
- Cinnamon stick – ½ inch
- Bay leaf – 1
- Scallions – 2, chopped, white and green parts separated

Other

- Carrots – 2, chopped
- Tomatoes – 2, chopped
- Fresh shitake – 2 oz. chopped
- Avocado oil for sautéing
- Cilantro garnish

Beef

- Beef shank – 1.2 lb. bone in
- Salt and ground pepper to taste

Stew seasonings

- Beef stock – 1/3 cup
- Coconut aminos – 2 tbsp.
- Five spice powder – ½ tsp.
- Coarse salt – ½ tsp.

Method

1. Season the beef shank with salt and pepper on all sides.
2. Mix well coconut aminos, beef stock, salt, and five-spice powder. set aside in a bowl.
3. Press sauté on your IP.
4. Add 1 tbsp. avocado oil and sear the beef for 3 minutes per side. Set aside.
5. Add more oil if necessary and sauté white scallion parts, bay leaf, cinnamon, chili pepper, ginger, garlic, and onion. Season with salt and pepper and sauté until fragrant. Press Cancel.

6. Scrape the bottom of the pot to remove any stuck bit.
7. Place beef on top of the aromatics.
8. Add shiitake, tomatoes, and carrots.
9. Seal and press Manual.
10. Cook on High for 45 minutes.
11. Wait 15 minutes then do a quick release.
12. Remove the beef and debone.
13. Add them back to the pot.
14. Garnish with cilantro and green scallion parts.
15. Serve over cauliflower rice.

Nutritional Facts Per Serving

- Calories: 289
- Fat: 7g
- Carb: 8g
- Protein: 40g

CONCLUSION

In this delightful Asian Instant Pot cookbook, you will learn to enjoy a variety of dishes that offer a wide range of flavors, textures, aromas, and colors. Designed for easy weeknight eating, this unique cookbook's wide range of dishes from a variety of Asian cuisines will appeal to all the home cooks. Each of these 130 recipes has been streamlined for home cooks of all experience levels. You don't have to order take outs anymore, just gather your ingredients, add them into your Instant Pot and an authentic Asian meal is ready within minutes! These recipes are sure to please picky eaters and gyoza connoisseurs alike! Impress friends and family with these satisfying and easy-to-make recipes.

Made in the USA
San Bernardino, CA
15 December 2019

61512545R00193